The Invisible Medal...

Stimulating! Chris brings spirit and evidence of what and why we do for our students, employees, and communities that we serve. Great read for those who lead or want to lead others. Proves successful leadership styles across all occupations. Focus on the individual, earn your invisible Medal.
    Jeff Lynn
    President, Central Alabama Community College

Colonel Chris Richie epitomizes the servant leader. Chris understands and practices a "Mission First; People Always" leadership philosophy, where success is achieved not by the "what" but by the "who." Chris knows our Country's most lethal weapon is the person wearing the cloth of our military, and taking care of those serving ensures success on the battlefield and success in life.
    Lieutenant General Michael Rocco USMC (Ret)
    President, Marines' Memorial Association & Foundation

Colonel Richie's vast experience in guiding Marines translates to every leader! He embodies the essence of a great American and exemplifies humility and thoughtfulness in leadership, steadfastly adhering to his values. His inspirational storytelling captivates his audience, leaving them asking for more. Our team found immense value in reflecting on our life and leadership crucibles, promoting a deeper examination of our purpose and priorities in leadership. Through introspection into our personal beliefs and their impact on our leadership styles, I discovered my own non-negotiables and found better ways to support my team.
    Lisa Hales
    Senior Vice President, All-in Credit Union

Chris delivers great insight into the fact that the visible rewards of leadership are neither the most valuable nor the most enduring. Those rewards are found in equipping others to succeed.
    Franklin Littleton
    President, Consumer North America, DHL Supply Chain (retired)

Colonel Chris Richie's values-based leadership approach, particularly the notion of earning Invisible Medals by helping others find their purpose and succeed, is at the heart of servant leadership. This book provides a profound opportunity for self-reflection and building one's own personal leadership purpose.
    Jennifer Mueller-Phillips, Ph.D.
    Interim Dean, Harbert College of Business, Auburn University

Colonel Richie's *The Invisible Medal* truly stands out among the multitude of leadership books available today, serving as a genuine game-changer. With masterful storytelling, Chris guides readers on a captivating journey of self-reflection, unraveling the essence of purpose in both life and leadership. A must-read for any established or aspiring leader!"
    Captain John Conrad
    Managing Director of Flight Line Operations East, American Airlines (retired)

The Invisible Medal

Leading with a Higher Purpose

Colonel Chris Richie
USMC, Retired

Next Chapter Publishing LLC
Inlet Beach, FL

Copyright © 2024 by Chris Richie

All rights reserved. No part of this publication may be reproduced, stored in retrieval systems, or transmitted in any form or by any means without prior written permission from the publisher. Moral rights asserted / All rights reserved.

Published by Next Chapter Publishing LLC, Inlet Beach, FL. www.nextchapterpublishing.net

The Invisible Medal: Leading with a Higher Purpose ©/ by Chris Richie. theinvisiblemedal.com

Cover design by: Kimberly Graham

The views expressed in this publication are those of the author and do not necessarily reflect the official policy or position of the Department of Defense or the U.S. government. The public release clearance of this publication by the Department of Defense does not imply Department of Defense endorsement or factual accuracy of the material. Cleared for open publication, Feb 29, 2024.

ISBN: 978-1-7358342-3-8

Other published works by Chris Richie:

1. "Leadership Lessons from Nicaragua." Marine Corps Gazette. Marine Corps Association. July 2020.

2. *The Ladybug's Gift.* Next Chapter Publishing LLC. March 2018.

3. "SPMAGTF Leaders in Action." Marine Corps Gazette. Marine Corps Association. August 2012.

4. *We Need War Principles for Our Generation.* Biblioscholar Dissertations. April 2005.

5. "We Need Functional Doctrine." Naval Proceedings. U.S. Naval Institute. September 2001.

6. "Try the TEAM Principle." Naval Proceedings. U.S. Naval Institute. July 2001.

7. "Warrant Officers to the Rescue." Marine Corps Gazette. Marine Corps Association. May 2001.

Acknowledgments

The Invisible Medal has been impacted by thousands of people over the course of my life-long leadership journey. My sincere appreciation to:

-Jesus, for teaching me how to be a humble servant leader.
-My wife, Michele, RPh, best friend, soulmate, true companion. Each of the 17 times I was ordered to move, she volunteered to move, to keep our family together, to embrace yet another adventure. She has earned countless Invisible Medals and makes everyone around her better.
-My daughters, Hannah, and Kate, for bringing me joy and happiness and making me a better version of myself.
-My parents. Gone but not forgotten. For teaching countless values, giving me the best childhood, and setting me on a path to achieve my potential.
-Grandpa Conrad, for your selfless service and helping me find my purpose.
-My brothers, Travis and Ryan for your friendship and encouragement.
-John and Margaret Conrad, for your mentorship, guidance, and unwavering support.
-My Aunts and Uncles, for teaching me the deep significance of family & faith.
-Ken Foster, for your early support and motivating me to pursue my passions.
-Ken Blanchard, for your sage advice and servant leadership.
-Matt Booker and San Diego Leadership Forum for your fellowship.
-Jennifer, Liesl, Jan, Meagan, Emma for believing in me and allowing me to teach and mentor Auburn University students.
-Bill, Hope, Jacob, and Kevin for paving the way for me to speak publicly.
-Kelli, Karla and the Human Resource Development Team, Kim, Penny, and Moriah for giving me purpose beyond the Marine Corps.

-Auburn University, Harbert College of Business, and University Human Resources for helping me fuel my passions.
-All-in Credit Union, Lisa, and Tara for the opportunity to speak to your team while motivating me to improve my work.
-All the leaders who mentored me and showed me the way.
-All the Marines who inspired me to be a better leader.
-My editors, Michele, John, Travis, and Ryan.
-To the authors I have quoted. Thank you for your inspiration and helping me "stand upon the shoulders of giants."
-The United States Marine Corps. I will be a Marine for life and aside from being called father and husband, "Marine" is one of my greatest honors.
-For the countless people who took the time to give me an invisible medal.

You are the reason this book was written!

Soli Deo Gloria

"To God alone, the glory"

Contents

	Introduction	13
Part One:	**Becoming a Servant Leader**	
Chapter 1:	The Invisible Medal	27
Chapter 2:	Finding Purpose	57
Chapter 3:	Finding Your Story	75
Chapter 4:	A Leadership Philosophy	89
Part Two:	**Leading with a Higher Purpose**	
Chapter 5:	Leadership	121
	Leader Development Continuum	131
Chapter 6:	Values	137
Chapter 7:	Ethics	161
Chapter 8:	Character	181
Part Three:	**Roots of Success**	
Chapter 9:	Culture	213
Chapter 10:	Marine Corps Culture	243
	Personal Culture	257
Appendix 1:	Questions for Reflection	265
Appendix 2:	Additional Notes and Reflection	267

Introduction

My leadership journey has been remarkable. There have been both joyful peaks and challenging valleys, yet every chapter of my life has been filled with learning and teaching moments. In 2015, I had the honor to represent the military during the San Diego National Prayer breakfast. Some of the people I met that day included TV/radio host Ken Foster and renowned leadership author, Ken Blanchard. A few years later, I found myself on a golf course with Mr. Blanchard who offered sage advice on writing a leadership book. His words still echo in my mind, "Chris, before you start your book, you need to ask yourself, what is it that you wish to teach?"

After a few years of reflection, I have found my answer. I want to share the story on how I became a servant leader in the hopes that others will be inspired to become a servant leader and make a difference in our world, one person at a time.

The Invisible Medal: Leading with a Higher Purpose is summarized below:

> **Invisible medals** will be earned if we focus on people and relationships, view life as a stewardship, and recognize that everyone has potential. Finding **our purpose** and **our story** comes from our life's **crucibles** and deep self-**reflection**. **Leadership** is personal. Your

definition will reveal both how you wish to be led and how you wish to lead. Knowing who we are helps determine our core **values** necessary to lead ourselves; Consistently making sound **ethical decisions** builds **trust** necessary to lead others; Consistently living in accordance with our values and sound ethical decisions yields habits that define our **character** which is necessary to effectively lead teams. Embracing the ethos that defines us and our organization's **culture** unleashes potential. Fully understanding your purpose, your unique story, personal values, and lessons from your life's crucibles will form a **leadership philosophy** that is unique to you. Holding yourself accountable to your philosophy will allow you to lead with authenticity.

Servant Leadership

Servant leadership has been around for thousands of years. For example, any parent who sacrificed for their child was a servant leader. Jesus discussed servant leadership when he said for anyone to lead, "they first must serve." [1] He epitomized servant leadership principles through his words and actions and left us with a final commandment to love one another. Throughout my life, I have often reflected on the word "love" and have come to realize "love" not only epitomizes the core principles of servant leadership, but also describes how we should treat everyone, regardless of their position or job title. In other words, "a leader" could replace the word "love" to describe the fundamental leadership traits we should embody.

Love (A Leader) …is patient and kind. Does not envy, does not boast, is not proud (vain). Does not dishonor others, is not self-seeking, is not easily angered, keeps no record of wrongs. Does not delight in evil but rejoices with the truth. Always protects, always trusts, always hopes, always perseveres. [2]

Servant Leader scholars know that Robert Greenleaf first coined the phrase servant leadership in 1970 with his article, "The Servant as Leader." He found inspiration for his concept from Hermann Hesse's book, *Journey to the East* where the servant Leo emerged as the true leader among heroes because he served the needs of others which helped them initially succeed in their journey. When Leo suddenly departed, the team of heroes failed. In a twist, Leo was the actual leader of the group who viewed himself first as the servant. For Robert Greenleaf, the message was clear, "the great leader is seen as servant first." [3]

Becoming an authentic and successful servant leader is much more than simply fulfilling the needs of those under your care. An authentic servant leader must first look inward to identify their foundational **purpose** and **values**. They must reflect on their life's **crucibles** and understand the leadership **philosophy** that has been born from those crucibles. When leadership dilemmas emerge, the servant leader can weather the storm because their principles have been built on solid ground. Questions you will consider throughout this book include, "What is your purpose? What is your story? What do you value most? What virtues guide your behavior and ethical decisions? How can you shape your unique story into serving others?

The Invisible Medal is written in the same manner as my keynote deliveries and how I teach at Auburn University which is via the Socratic method. Socrates was a well-known philosopher who espoused teaching via multiple questions to take the listener on a journey inward. He would say, "I cannot teach anyone anything, but I can make them think." [4] My objective will be to present leadership theory with a heavy dose of leadership practice followed by personal reflection for the reader to think and to document answers to specific questions that will help you develop your own purpose, your story, your personal leadership philosophy.

Storytelling

Anyone who has ever seen a Ted Talk will understand the power of storytelling. In the book, *Ted Talks: The Official TED Guide to Public Speaking,* author Chris Anderson opines that

Introduction

"Human to human communication is a true wonder of the world." Chris further conveys that following a good story, "…a little piece of you has become a little piece of them (the listener) …People love stories." [5] Humans have interacted with one another for thousands of years through stories. Long before the written word existed, people conveyed knowledge through the spoken voice. Humans learned long ago that the best means to captivate an audience, a child, or a friend was by telling a story.

Equally powerful is the knowledge gained from our life experiences. Some experiences are tragic such as my grandfather who endured the Bataan Death March and over three years as a prisoner of war during World War II. Other experiences are beautiful, such as watching our child take their first steps in this world. We learn from our experiences. These experiences teach us to appreciate the life we have, to repeat behaviors that bring us joy and—when possible—avoid behaviors that bring us grief.

Military servicemen and women have experienced incredible events which were life-altering. Most of us keep those experiences to ourselves falsely believing that only fellow servicemen and women will understand our stories. I have learned that American citizens have deep pride in our Nation and are thankful for our armed forces and especially for our citizens who volunteer to serve. They want to hear more of our stories, and we should uphold that desire.

The military refers to such methodology as "Sea Stories" and most service members I know are masters at telling them. In each chapter, I will be extremely transparent with personal stories over a lifetime of good and bad examples of learning to lead. In essence, my methodology will be to "teach" through storytelling and reflection.

Reflection

In 1933, American philosopher and education reformer John Dewey reminded us that "We do not learn from experience... we learn from reflecting on experience." [6] So many events happen to us every day. They will simply remain white noise until we pause, think, reflect, and learn from them. For example, **I do my best thinking when I am not thinking**. Sounds strange, but I wager many can relate. Oftentimes, when I have difficulty solving a problem, I will go for a jog and free my mind from everything...no stocks, no politics, no social media, nothing but me, nature, and my heavy breathing. Before long, an idea or a thought will emerge which lights my path to solving a problem. As mentioned, throughout *The Invisible Medal* will be several thought-provoking questions with plenty of room on the page for the reader to reflect and write down responses.

Self-reflection is an absolute requirement to unlock the hidden leadership potential in all of us.

The Marine Corps ingrains 14 specific leadership traits and 11 leadership principles into the memory of every Marine. One has always stood out which is to "Know yourself and seek self-improvement." [7] Thirty-four years later, I still reflect to better know myself and constantly seek ways to improve. The opposite of knowing yourself is best articulated by Lewis Carrol when he opined that if you don't know where you are going, any road will get you there. [8] Although typically quoted to emphasize why a vision statement for organizations is so important, Carrol's statement also applies to leading oneself. For example, anyone not grounded in personal values can easily find themselves on the road of convenience versus the road of principle.

You cannot authentically lead with a higher purpose if you do not know what you believe in.

Once a person spends time to reflect and unlock the doors in their subconscious to reveal their personal values/beliefs and deep-rooted assumptions/bias, they will be free to lead with purpose and authenticity. My theory on purposeful leadership will be consistent for every reader; however, the practice and personal message will be perceived differently because everyone is unique with different life experiences and crucibles that have defined who we are.

Purpose

My purpose is to help individuals and teams achieve their full potential through authentic servant leadership. Ideally, I hope to inspire servant leaders around the globe to make a positive difference by investing in people and relationships. *The Invisible Medal* will explain how a person's leadership potential can be unleashed through self-reflection. Reflection helps us understand our purpose, our story, our values, our character, our leadership philosophy, and our own personal culture. The life events that have formed us into the person that makes us uniquely unique must be understood before we can truly become a servant leader and inspire others. By applying knowledge about ourselves, we transform our personal experiences into how to lead with authenticity.

- We lead effectively if we lead authentically.
- We lead authentically if we understand and articulate who we are, what we believe, and why we believe it.
- The best way to articulate those beliefs is through a personal leadership philosophy, crafted from our life's experiences and crucibles.

The Invisible Medal focuses on the key attributes vital to developing your personal leadership philosophy. My leadership philosophy is **T-E-A-M-S**, which was derived after years of

Introduction

cultivating personal values, ethical behavior, character, and a personal culture. T-E-A-M-S stands for <u>T</u>rain, <u>E</u>mpower, <u>A</u>cknowledge, <u>M</u>entor, and <u>S</u>erve. [9] This philosophy has helped me understand that holding ourselves accountable to our values and beliefs helps us gain the trust and confidence of those we are privileged to lead. To succeed requires time and effort and above all, true understanding of who we are.

- To lead others, you must first learn to lead yourself.
- To lead a team, you must learn to lead others.
- To lead an organization, you must first learn to lead a team.

Method

As we grow and lead at higher levels, we must have a strong foundation built on personal **values**. Once we have codified our core values, we can manifest those values through **ethical behavior**, followed by our consistent habits which define our **character**, and finally an ethos that can shape personal and organizational **culture**. Although I share several stories from my 30 years of active-duty military service and leadership development at institutions of higher education (Auburn University and the Air War College), this book is not intended to provide a template on how I performed as a servant leader. Rather, my goal is to help you discover your leadership potential within and how your values, behavior, character, and personal culture can help you lead with a higher purpose.

21

In essence, our path is one of self-discovery. **You have the power within to be extraordinary.** Finding that internal power will be revealed through 30 self-discovery questions throughout this entire book. Here is your first question.

1. What would you like people to say about you as their leader?

_____
_____
_____
_____
_____
_____
_____
_____
_____
_____
_____
_____
_____
_____
_____
_____

End State

My strong hope is that *The Invisible Medal* becomes your personal leadership guidebook that is kept in your office or at home for quick reference. We are so busy in today's world and constantly bombarded by unlimited interruptions, so perhaps this book can help:

- Ground you in who you are.
- Determine what matters most to you as a leader.
- Understand how you can hold yourself accountable for what you believe and how you wish to lead.

I am excited to share my stories with you and wish you all the best on your life-long leadership journey. Let's Begin!

Notes:

1. Bible, New King James Version. Matthew 20:26-28. "Whoever desires to become great among you, let him be your servant."
2. 1 Corinthians 13:4-7. James Hunter also describes love as leadership in his book, *The Servant*, 1998.
3. Robert K. Greenleaf. *Servant Leadership, A Journey into the Nature of Legitimate Power & Greatness.* (New Jersey: Paulist Press, 1979).
4. https://www.goodreads.com/quotes/73059-i-cannot-teach-anybody-anything-i-can-only-make-them.
5. Chris Anderson. *Ted Talks, The Official TED Guide to Public Speaking.* Harcourt Publishing Company, New York, New York. 2016.
6. John Dewey. https://ecampusontario.pressbooks.pub/reflectivepracticeinearlyyears/chapter/3-2-beginning-theories/.
7. USMC Company Commander's Notebook. Marine Corps Institute, Arlington, VA. 1989.
8. Lewis Carroll, *Alice's Adventures in Wonderland* (New York: Macmillan, 1865).
9. Chris S. Richie. "Try the TEAM Principle". U.S. Naval Institute Proceedings. July 2001. https://www.usni.org/magazines/proceedings/2001/july/try-team-principle.

Part One

Photo of author during pre-deployment training at Camp LeJeune, 2010

Becoming a Servant Leader

The Invisible Medal

Chapter One

The Invisible Medal

"A Soldier will fight long and hard
for a bit of colored ribbon."
-Napoleon

Human nature drives us to succeed. From an early age, we are told that we are either below average, average, or above average. This is evident in our early report cards and placement on sports teams. Each time we earn an "A" in school, or a starting position in sports, we feel successful. On the other hand, anything below an "A" or being a "bench-warmer," sends us countless negative messages. Those messages could be, "I missed the mark; I can't do this, or worst yet, I guess I will never be a success in school or in sports." In sports, the best teams receive trophies and accolades. Just as with school, becoming successful in sports requires hard work, commitment, and perseverance. Once we enter the work force, these virtues reward us with promotions, bonus checks, merit pay, and exceptional performance reviews.

For those serving in the military, competition for promotion is extremely high. Excellence is rewarded with medals and ribbons proudly worn on our uniforms. The famous French Commander, Napoleon understood the sacrifices people are willing to endure simply to earn what he called, "…a bit of colored ribbon." [1]

I will never forget the time I earned my first "ribbon." Although I really did not earn the National Defense Service Medal (given to anyone on active duty during Operation Desert Storm), I was so happy to have something on my chest. At least until I—along with every Second Lieutenant—was ridiculed for wearing something that had not been earned. Most of us had not even completed basic training when the medal was authorized. I recall a cartoon joke making rounds throughout

the Marine Corps of an older enlisted man pointing to a Lieutenant's chest and his sole ribbon with the caption, "Hey sir, you have a pizza stain on your uniform." [2] There is always a fundamental truth in humor, and I was honestly embarrassed. As a young Lieutenant, I felt I had an uphill battle to prove that I was a leader worth following.

At a young age, military culture focuses us to be aware of our own accomplishments, simply because we believe our awards will determine if we get promoted, thus allowing us to continue serving our nation and leading Marines. Aside from military promotions, the most visible representation of a service-member's success (or lack thereof) is revealed by the ribbons and medals worn on their uniform. In other words, the number of ribbons and medals on your chest is directly proportional to the success you have achieved (or so I once thought). In essence, a service-member wears their military biography on their chest for all to see. A quick glance will tell the observer what military operations that person has participated in, how many times they have been deployed, how many times they have been decorated for heroism in combat, and how many times they have been recognized for superior performance. For some, they are proud to flaunt their military record with excessive pride; for others, they are embarrassed for not achieving more accolades. Regardless, it is unfortunate that such truths only enhance an already highly competitive profession. To be fair, there are several people who are humble and have achieved such a high level of self-actualization that they only wear ribbons and medals as required and simply do not pay much attention to their past achievements. For these individuals, their focus is elsewhere which is serving others.

I had been active duty for fourteen years when I finally realized just how insignificant medals are when compared to the greatest reward in having the opportunity to serve others; to help people achieve their full potential; to be there when they need you the most (marriage issues, career decisions, physical, mental, and spiritual growth).

When you make a difference in someone's life and they acknowledge you for that impact, you have earned the most valuable of all medals, The Invisible Medal.

No one sees it. You do not wear it on your chest. Only you and the person you influenced know it exists. And there is nothing more important than the Invisible Medal. It does not matter who we are, where we work, what our title is; EVERYONE can earn the Invisible Medal. My journey to this realization started in the Middle East.

Mission Top Secret; Destination Unknown

I vividly recall the day the world changed on September 11th, 2001. As a Company Commander, I had the privilege to provide a tour of our long-range radar and air defense capability to the new Marine Expeditionary Force (MEF) Commander, a three star General. Our tour was cut short when the General's aide interrupted us and whisked our VIP away in a rush. Upon entering our building, I noticed a large crowd of Marines huddled around the duty hut trying to get a peek at the television. I asked what was going on. One of our Marines said, "Sir, a plane just flew into the world trade center." I immediately asked myself, how could someone be so dumb to accidentally fly a small plane into such a large building? Then, we watched, along with millions of other viewers around the globe, as a second plane flew into the other world trade center building. All of us huddled around the duty hut knew our nation was under attack. Upon hearing the news anchor report other hijacked planes were in the air, we directed our radars to power up and play any role we could to help defend our homeland. Our radar, the TPS-59 is a long-range radar used by the Marine Corps to control aircraft and surface-to-air missiles. Although New York City was well outside our range, Washington D.C was just barely within range. As the next several minutes unfolded, we were bewildered, angry, and shocked, but hyper focused. It was eerie that our radar was completely "clean," meaning no aircraft were flying, something we had never seen before. Occasionally we would identify aircraft and pass that information to the Southeast Air Defense

Sector (our normal administrative reporting chain had been significantly changed in an instant). At one point, some Marine operators overheard background chatter about Air Force One being airborne to which I thought, good Lord, we are at War.

Less than three months later, we had a deployment order, a classified mission and location so secret that only a select few individuals knew where we were going. Imagine telling a group of 135 Marines to be prepared for any contingency, for a long-term deployment in a classified location. It was no surprise that everyone loved it. We sing cadences to such things, but never expected to live it.

C-130 Rolling down the strip.
U.S. Marines gonna take a little trip.
Mission top secret, destination unknown.
I don't know when I'm coming home.

After a pre-deployment site survey, I was designated the Commanding Officer for the Tactical Air Operations Center (TAOC)-Reinforced which called for four platoons, three of which had to be sourced throughout II Marine Expeditionary Force (MEF), Marines with whom I had never met. We had two months to prepare. One of our platoons was designated the Security Platoon, responsible for 24/7 security. None of them were infantry professionals, but "Every Marine is a rifleman," and all were up to the challenge. I will never forget one very late evening in my office. I was frustrated by still needing two Marines to complete the roster for our security platoon and with just a few days away from our deployment, I was beginning to lose hope. Just then, I heard a knock on my door. In perfect unison, two Marines requested to enter, marched in step to the prescribed 18 inches from my desk, jumped to attention and forcefully announced, "Sir, Lance Corporal Lamb and Lance Corporal Koshuta reporting as ordered." After placing them at ease, I asked what unit they were from. Simultaneously, both Marines stated, **"We're in the Band sir!"** Admittingly, I believe I laughed out loud, as they both smirked, recognizing how that must have sounded. I then asked if they knew anything about our deployment to which they said no. When I inquired as to how they came to not only learn about the deployment but also to have volunteered, they revealed the band director told the entire unit that we needed two volunteers to deploy to an unknown location for an unknown period, to serve in a classified mission directed by the Secretary of Defense. Of course, I figured they were the only volunteers; however, I was nearly brought to tears when they said, "No sir, EVERYONE volunteered. We were the lucky ones to have been chosen." No matter what I had felt up until that point, I was unbelievably inspired by their courage and patriotism. I promised myself that evening that I would give everything I had, and more to ensure a successful mission and that I would bring everyone back home alive and well. The following week, we departed the safety of the United States and embarked on our own "journey to the East", excited, well-prepared, and anxious.

Members of TAOC-Reinforced, 2002

Seven months later, our mission was complete. During our time together on such a small base, we all got to know one another extremely well. I will never forget how impressed I was with the level of patriotism, teamwork, and commitment by all our Marines. Several of our teammates, such as Jon Koshuta, Jimmy Clevenger, and James Wuestman were such exceptional leaders that I often had conversations with them about their potential to become a Marine Corps officer.

Multiple VIPs had visited our base, which we named Camp Scorpion. One such VIP was none other than the U.S. Central Command Commander, General Tommy Franks. Near the end of our deployment, he had stated our Marines' performance was "Flawlessly Executed." In keeping with "a bit of colored ribbon" concept, I ensured that everyone was acknowledged with some form of appreciation ranging from a letter of appreciation up to Joint Service Commendation Medals. Other commanders within the region received Bronze Stars, so I was eagerly awaiting my recognition, which after several months, I came to realize, would never come. I wondered about my future promotion opportunities and the potential negative message that was being sent fearing that no recognition for my seven-month deployment might be a way to say that I was a bad leader. Such thoughts took me to a place of bitterness. In honest transparency, I was disillusioned; however, I was also reminded of the "better versus bitter" story shared during a command visit from our higher headquarters. The Group Chaplain, Chaplain Forneau, gave a motivational talk about putting ourselves in the right frame of mind when we experience hardship and "rather than becoming bitter, just focus on being better." One letter in the alphabet (I versus E), can make a significant difference in our outlook on life. His story helped me get over myself and reframe my perspective. A few years later, I received the following e-mail from then-Lance Corporal Koshuta's wife, Beth (also at the time serving as a Marine):

Sir,

As you know this year's MECEP and BOOST orders finally came out and my husband has been accepted! It has been four years since you planted the idea in his head, but you are the reason he started the process in the first place. Thank you so much for your leadership and the influence that you have had on him. We have worked with entirely too many leaders unworthy of emulation in our time in the Corps and I am so grateful that he has had the opportunity to work for a Marine like you.

We are very excited about starting this new chapter in our lives. I'll be taking terminal leave in August when he leaves for the prep school in Rhode Island and from there we are planning for Penn State. I should be finishing my bachelor's degree through University of Phoenix around that time and am thrilled at the thought of following him wherever he goes and seeking employment that allows me to support his career. Leaving him at home while I'm out here just doesn't feel quite right.

At retirement ceremonies there is a letter read that always references the "many Marines you have influenced" and I feel it important to let you know that your influence on our lives has been immeasurable. Thank you for all that you have done for us and for being the kind of Marine that we can look up to.

This e-mail dropped me like a sack of potatoes and instantly changed everything I knew regarding what success really means. Napoleon was right in terms of people desiring to be acknowledged, but I had discovered something far more meaningful than a piece of ribbon. What I discovered was…

True fulfillment comes when you positively impact another person's life.

Success is irrelevant when compared to influence and significance.

The Invisible Medal concept was born and this kindhearted e-mail from a Marine's spouse was my first invisible medal. My personal success, awards, promotions, and ribbons no longer mattered; rather, helping others achieve their potential became my passion, and remains so today.

The invisible medals I wear in my heart vastly outshine those visible medals I once wore on my chest.

Servant leaders understand our experience in life is not just about us; it is about everyone, and if we can make a difference in someone's life, we are called to do so. In the book, *Halftime*, author Bob Buford expertly explains why significance is so much more important than success, especially in our life's "second half." [3]. Seeking significance is the servant leaders calling. Servant leaders hear this calling to serve something greater than themselves; **Serving others is the greatest calling**. This epiphany will help people graduate from Maslow's hierarchy of human needs, catapult us from self-actualization, and flip Maslow's pyramid upside down. [4] Our new focus is on others, to help them grow, achieve their full potential, and become self- actualized, so they too can become servant leaders.

Visible medals = Success
Invisible Medals = Significance

I am reminded of the quote in Proverbs which states, "The generous will prosper; those who refresh others will themselves be refreshed." [5] The rewards from earning invisible medals are immeasurable because servant leaders understand their calling and are most content when fulfilling their purpose; To make a difference by helping others achieve their full potential!

2. **Have you earned any Invisible Medals by positively influencing another human being? If so, who was it and what did you do for them?**

_____
_____
_____
_____
_____
_____
_____
_____
_____
_____
_____
_____

Equally important to earning invisible medals is taking the time to give invisible medals, and it is so easy for us to do. How many times has someone gone out of their way for us? How many people have sacrificed something because we were in need? When others positively impact us, we should send them a note or tell them in person just how thankful we are for their positive impact. One of my favorite movies, *Woodlawn*, plays out a powerful moment when a high school football coach (Tandy Gerelds) receives a phone call from a former player (Tony Nathan). During the scene, Tony, who just won the College Football National Championship with the University of Alabama under legendary head coach "Bear" Bryant, calls his former High School Football coach to celebrate the victory. Tony learns that Tandy is no longer coaching when Tony encourages him to return to his calling because he was the "best coach I ever had." [6] What an invisible medal to give someone! Tandy's commitment and service to his players was significant; and Tony's phone call is likely what motivated him to return to coaching, inspiring hundreds of people and earning a state championship.

To further illustrate, consider the classic Christmas movie, *It's a Wonderful Life*. The character George Bailey is given a gift to see how the world would have turned out had he never been born. What George learns is that he truly lived a life of great significance impacting hundreds of lives and truly living a wonderful life. George Bailey earned countless Invisible Medals because his guardian angel, Clarence chose to show him. [7] I am certain there are countless people just like George Bailey who have had a significant impact on many people's lives; it is so important we take the time to let them know.

3. **Has anyone done something for you that positively impacted your life? If so, write down their names and what they did for you. Then, send them an e-mail or give them a call to let them know.**

_____
_____
_____
_____
_____
_____
_____
_____
_____
_____
_____
_____
_____
_____
_____
_____
_____
_____

Earning and giving invisible medals requires a servant leader's heart and can be made easy if we:

- **Focus on people and relationships.**
- **View life as a stewardship.**
- **Recognize that everyone has potential.**

People and Relationships

Servant leaders naturally focus on others first. They have matured from inward (self) focused to outward (others) focused. Servant leaders ensure needs are met and people are enabled to achieve their full potential. As a junior officer, I certainly focused on the Marines under my charge. "Looking out for your Marines and their welfare" is a core Marine Corps principle. However, deep down, I was also focused on being a successful Marine. My Military Occupational Specialty (MOS) was highly technical which required significant study and training. The paradigm I experienced was a never-ending internal tug of war being both self-focused and others focused. Servant leaders learn to handle this dilemma by measuring their success through the success achieved by those entrusted to their care. Maslow's hierarchy describes the levels of personal needs culminating with self-actualization. I have often wondered what comes after self-actualization and now realize, the next step is to focus on others, helping people rise through Maslow's hierarchy ultimately achieving their own self-actualization. [8]

When the servant leader helps another person achieve self-actualization, they will have earned an invisible medal.

We are so caught up in the number of Instagram followers or Facebook friends, but how many of those "friends" do we truly know? How many of those social media "friends" do we have a meaningful relationship with? I fear today's technology is taking us away from fostering meaningful relationships; perhaps taking us away from those investments that produce invisible medals. Servant leaders understand that time is the greatest treasure. Time combined with mentorship, empathy, and passion to help others are the most valuable commodity to building relationships and forming bonds of trust. It is not the accumulation of things or wealth that matters, but rather people and relationships that matter most. Herin lies the greatest treasure. Renowned author and priest Henri Nouwen captured this sentiment perfectly when he revealed that he used to get annoyed by people who constantly interrupted his work until the day he realized, the people are his work. [9]

Helping others starts with genuinely understanding them and being attuned to their specific circumstances. The military calls this the "human factors" that determine alignment and success or struggle and failure. This requires one-on-one discussions referred to as a Supervisor/Direct Report meeting or a Counseling session in the military. Unfortunately, all too often, these meetings solely focus on the individual's job performance, while overlooking the areas which matter most. Servant leaders will focus on more than just job performance; they will focus on all aspects that matter to the individual such as physical, mental, family, spiritual, and community. I call these our **Life Pillars**. Everyone has a different set of life pillars, and goals associated with those pillars. Perhaps they want to be a Sunday school teacher, or write a children's book, or own a bookstore, travel to Europe, buy their first home, run a marathon, compete in an Olympic trial, spend time with their grandkids, or get married and start a family. Just as every human has potential, every Servant Leader has an opportunity to make a difference to help people achieve their personal and professional goals within their individual life pillars. Their opportunity lies at the threshold of seeing people as unique, full of ambition and desires, not just a simple employee with a job to do. Supervisors will never know what their employee's priorities and goals are until they ask. These open discussions produce a very welcomed side effect—Trust.

Supervisors who listen and care can lighten someone's burden and remove barriers that keep them from achieving their goals.

As such, employees will look forward to your one-on-one meetings. At some point, they will tell you how you helped them achieve a personal or professional goal. When that happens, congratulations, you just earned an invisible medal.

4. **Have you ever helped someone overcome a hardship or achieve a goal? Explain the circumstances. How did it make you feel?**

_____
_____
_____
_____
_____
_____
_____
_____
_____
_____
_____
_____
_____
_____
_____
_____
_____
_____
_____
_____
_____
_____

So many companies operate from a position of fear over losing employees with a focus on performance and profit. This logic typically backfires, resulting in employees seeking relationships and growth opportunities elsewhere. In April 2022, McKinsey and Company released a report on exit interview trends which was so alarming, the term "The Great Resignation" emerged. The top reason why employees quit in 2021 was because they did not feel valued by the organization. [10] Everyone serves a vital purpose within every organization. Just as a small missing tile for a beautiful mosaic is readily noticed, people serve to complete our teams and organizations. It is critically important for leaders to recognize that everyone not only brings value to the organization, but they also bring value outside of the office, for their families, clubs, friends, church groups, etc.

It is so important to balance our priorities and life pillars. When not balanced, our body and mind operate like a car that is out of alignment. Just like all the intricate components a vehicle requires to function properly, so does the human body, requiring alignment of mind, body, and soul for optimal performance. Servant leaders take time to understand the unique circumstances of others and serve their needs across the full spectrum of their personal life pillars. People will have different priorities and motivators. We should recognize those differences and do all we can to help them be successful in all their life pillars. This is life alignment, and the happier employees are with those pillars, the happier they will be in both their personal and professional lives.

Closely tied to life pillars are personal priorities. Everyone has their own set of priorities. Leaders should never coerce someone to deviate from their personal priorities. We should stop focusing solely on work priorities and start lending a helping hand in life priorities. My priorities for the last 30 years have been God, Family, Country, Marine Corps. My new priorities are God, Family, People, Country. I have been fortunate (for the most part) to have leaders who did not ask me to compromise my priorities. One of my favorite movies growing up was *Chariots of Fire*. I was so inspired by the Scottish athlete, Eric Liddell. Although his calling was to pursue missionary work, he had a talent which was running, very fast. His dilemma was in choosing the right calling. Thankfully, he chose both and would pursue missionary work after the Olympics. A favorite to win the 100-meter race during the Paris Olympics in 1924, Liddell withdrew from the race because the qualifying heat was scheduled on a Sunday, in direct conflict with his top priority. The movie inspirationally portrays Liddell's challenges with a decision for which he was resolute and uncompromising. Instead of being angry with his decision, a fellow teammate gave up his event for Liddell where he ran the 400-meter race, winning Gold and setting an Olympic record which stood for 12 years. [11] This movie taught me how important it is to not only follow our calling, but more importantly, the honor that can come from preserving what matters most, your priorities.

Stewardship

Throughout my military career, I have attended countless "change of command" ceremonies symbolizing the transfer of command from one officer to another. The pomp and circumstance of these ceremonies is impressive, complete with a band, military formations, speeches, and a "pass in review."

Although there is no rule on how long the speeches should be, the incoming commander keeps remarks brief, 2-3 minutes, while the outgoing commander keeps their remarks to less than 10 minutes, so they do not cause unnecessary discomfort to the personnel standing in formation. At almost every single change of command, one or both speakers will talk about the "stewardship of command." Webster's defines stewardship as "the careful and responsible management of something entrusted to one's care." **Most commanders view their time in command as sacred and entrusted to their care for a short period of time.**

Commanding Officers understand their time in command is finite, anywhere from 18-24 months; not long to make an impact, to truly get to know people and provide the leadership they and their families deserve, or to accomplish the organizational mission, while improving the lives of those under their charge. Simply put, **to leave the command in better shape than they found it.** Those who truly excel will not only achieve that worthy goal, but they will also leave behind a **legacy.** They will have impacted lives in such a way to have inspired them to be the best versions of themselves. Commanders understand their stewardship is not about them; it is all about their organization and the people who run it. World War I military hero, author, and retired Marine LtCol John Thomason accurately captured this sentiment.

> ...a column represents a great deal more than 28,000 individuals mustered into a division. All that is behind those men is in that column too: the old battles, long forgotten, that secured our nation ... traditions of things endured, and things accomplished, **such as regiments hand down forever**; and the faith of men and the love of women; and that abstract thing called patriotism. [12]

Those who have been inspired and positively changed will pass along the leadership traits and principles observed in their commander who left a lasting impression. I have been greatly honored and privileged to command several times during my career and was both pleased and sad each time I handed our organizational colors to another commander. Pleased to know I always gave my best for the Marines and families I tried to positively influence; sad, because I know how much I will miss the opportunity to influence. During our change of command receptions, I would often be asked what I wished to do next to which my immediate response was "Anything that will allow me to be a commander again."

Since our time in command is short, the seeds planted in terms of initiatives we start, and our investments in people will not produce fruit until long after we have departed. In the book, *Legacy*, by James Kerr, the author refers to this mindset as "being a good ancestor." That you "do not own the jersey, you are just the body in the jersey at this time." Kerr also reminds us of the Greek proverb which honors old men who plant trees whose shade they will never see. [13] Commanders who are servant leaders do not care who gets the credit; only to know that they made a difference, that they have earned invisible medals. The best description of legacy for a servant leader is to see people succeed and achieve the full potential you saw in them and helped cultivate.

Since my military retirement, I have found a strong comparison between the stewardship of Command and what I call **the stewardship of life**. Life is a stewardship because human life is sacred and something special that has been entrusted to our care.

Every human has been given the gift of life.

What we do with our life is our gift to humanity.

Much like the finite period of command, life is also finite. Whether we live for 20, 40, or 80 years, how did we steward those years? If our time is spent investing in others, helping people achieve their full potential, earning invisible medals, then I believe you leave behind a legacy far more valuable than any savings account. Life is a book full of chapters, some more exciting than others, but when we are gone, the book remains. What will matter most is not the money we leave behind but rather the positive influence we had on the lives of others. How many invisible medals we earned.

No one will remember the medals we wore in life; but they will remember the impact we had on their life.

Arthur Ashe best articulated this sentiment when he stated, "You make a living from what you get, but make a life from what you give." [14] If every person viewed life the same way as a commander views their short time in command, our world would be a better place. People would understand that all life is important and has purpose. Leaders who endeavor to earn invisible medals will find the potential in everyone they encounter, they will focus on building meaningful relationships, and they will view life as a stewardship. They will learn the lesson from the ghost, Jacob Marley in *A Christmas Carol*, who so aptly stated, "Mankind was my business. The common welfare was my business; charity, mercy, forbearance, and benevolence, were all my business." [15] Achieving this level of self-actualization is a continuous journey which begins when we recognize that every human has potential.

Every Human has Potential

Every human is born with at least one thing in common, Potential. Have you ever been inspired by stories of people who overcame incredible odds to achieve greatness? A common denominator in most of these stories is that they had a mentor, someone who recognized their potential and devoted time to help them achieve their potential. There is such strong potential in every human being. That potential will lie dormant until a leader comes along who can ignite the spark and inspire them. Somewhere in the halls, offices, or cubicles of your organization is a person who could become a President, an inventor, a professional athlete, a servant leader. That same person can take what they have learned from you and pay it forward to another person, thus unleashing potential in others and positively impacting our world.

Clearly, not everyone will become the next Einstein or President; however, everyone—with the right mentor—can achieve their full potential. Servant leaders view every person in their organization as unique, and full of dormant potential. Observe, I used the word everyone. Not just those we think are high performing, high potential individuals, but everyone.

Everyone can be a high potential performer if they have the right leader.

We have too many labels placed upon us by society. There should be only one label, human. Many of our nation's problems can end when we realize that all souls look the same and every human has potential and a purpose. Servant leaders who selflessly mentor others can truly make this world a better place.

During our deployment, it was clear that Lance Corporal Koshuta was an exceptional leader who quickly rose through the ranks and earned positions of greater responsibility. An accomplished musician, he took the initiative to have his family heirloom bugle shipped to our remote location so he could play taps for our team every night. This simple gesture not only uplifted our spirits, but also served as a reminder of our purpose and mission. There was little doubt that he had a desire to serve and to lead others, which guaranteed his acceptance into the highly competitive Marine Corps Enlisted Commissioning Education Program (MECEP). Although my first conversation with him on the subject was quickly dismissed, I persisted. I endeavored to have similar meaningful conversations with all those under my charge and never knew if I had a breakthrough moment, which makes Jon's wife's e-mail even more powerful.

When you make a difference in someone's life, they will carry that positive energy home to their families, to their friends, their co-workers, members of their church or kid's soccer team. Your positive influence will lead them to influence others and in no time, there will be an entire wake of positive energy created just because you took the time to make an investment in one person. This is perhaps the greatest of any pyramid scheme ever to be created…and we all win. John Maxwell stated that "If you want to improve your world, then focus your attention on helping others." [16] This is so profoundly true. For example,

If 100 people reading this book are inspired to make a positive impact on just one person each month, that is 1,200 people who will be inspired this year.

If those 1,200 do the same and the cycle continues for four years, <u>2,073,600</u> people will be positively impacted as a direct result of servant leaders focused on helping others.

That is indeed changing the world. Let's do this together! One person at a time.

Notes:

1. Napoleon. https://www.brainyquote.com/quotes/napoleon_bonaparte_108401
2. Semper Toons cartoon. https://www.sempertoons.com/
3. Bob Buford. Halftime, Moving from Success to Significance. Zondervan, Grand Rapids, Michigan. 2008.
4. Maslow's hierarchy of needs is an idea in psychology proposed by American psychologist Abraham Maslow in his 1943 paper "A Theory of Human Motivation" in the journal Psychological Review.
5. Bible, New International Version. Proverbs 11:25.
6. *Woodlawn*. Pure Flix Entertainment. 2015.
7. *It's a Wonderful Life*. Liberty Films.1946.
8. Maslow's hierarchy of needs.
9. Henri Nouwen. https://henrinouwen.org/
10. McKinsey and Company. McKinsey Quarterly. "Great Attrition or Great Attraction? The Choice is Yours." September 2021. https://www.mckinsey.com/.
11. *Chariots of Fire*. Twentieth Century Fox, 1981. Also, https://en.wikipedia.org/wiki/Eric_Liddell.
12. John Tomason. *Jeb Stewart*. 1930.
13. James Kerr. *Legacy, What the All Blacks Can Teach us about the Business of Life*. Constable, London, England. 2013. The author describes how the All-Blacks rugby team from New Zealand became one of the best sports franchises in history.
14. Arthur Ashe. https://www.brainyquote.com/authors/arthur-ashe-quotes. This quote has also been attributed to Winston Churchill.
15. Charles Dickens. *A Christmas Carol*. Film adaptation, CBS. 1984. Also quoted from Charles Dickens original manuscript, A Christmas Carol. 1843.
16. John C. Maxwell. *How Successful People Think*. Center Street. 2009.

Finding Purpose

Major Eugene Conrad, 1948

Chapter Two

Finding Purpose

"The two most important days in a person's life are the day they are born and the day they discover why."
- Mark Twain

Most memories of my youth have faded; however, a few significant people and events stand out which shaped my upbringing and helped me discover my purpose. My Grandfather had an enormous impact on my early life. The preceding photo was taken just three years after he was liberated from a Japanese prisoner of war camp. He stood out as a man of honor and was a source of inspiration during my formative years. Additionally, "growing up" in the great state of Texas and my connection to Auburn University have played crucial roles in helping me discover my purpose. This chapter encapsulates the essence of discovering purpose and the impact it can have on your life. As you read the following chapter, consider the events in your life that helped you discover your passions, desires, goals, and hopes as you find your own purpose.

A Man of Honor

As a young child, I held my grandfather in the highest regard. He embodied the values of family, faith, patience, and kindness, all traits I wanted to emulate. He was not only my greatest mentor, but also a member of the "greatest generation" describing the men and women who preserved democracy during World War II and truly made America great. [1] My Grandfather's voice still echoes in my mind carrying words of wisdom.

> Always hope for the best, but be prepared for the worst. Never give up on your faith or hope. Serve a cause greater than yourself. Always give your best. Whatever your job happens to be, focus your energy to be the best at that job there ever was. Be slow to anger. Be a contributing citizen to our great nation.

During my teenage years, I spent much of my summers at the beach house he and my grandmother bought before

Finding Purpose

Destin, Florida became the vacation destination it is today. In fact, my grandparents designed and built the beach house thus fulfilling a life-long dream. They had six children and 27 grandchildren who gathered every other summer for family reunions. Over the years, I met several of grandpa's Army friends from his time in service and was always moved by the deep bonds of brotherhood, patriotism, and camaraderie they shared. I remember several family trips to Daleville, Alabama where my grandfather taught me how to fish, the joy of reading, and the simplicity of nature. I was amazed with his large home office full of military knick-naks; although in my youth, I never

> TO MEMBERS OF UNITED STATES ARMED FORCES BEING REPATRIATED IN OCTOBER 1945:
>
> It gives me special pleasure to welcome you back to your native shores, and to express, on behalf of the people of the United States, the joy we feel at your deliverance from the hands of the enemy. It is a source of profound satisfaction that our efforts to accomplish your return have been successful.
>
> You have fought valiantly in foreign lands and have suffered greatly. As your Commander in Chief, I take pride in your past achievements and express the thanks of a grateful Nation for your services in combat and your steadfastness while a prisoner of war.
>
> May God grant each of you happiness and an early return to health.
>
> *Harry Truman*

knew just how significant those items were such as a signed letter from President Truman.

During a change of command ceremony at Fort Rucker, Alabama (Now called Fort Novosel), I witnessed active-duty General Officers saluting my grandfather who had been retired for nearly a decade. Clearly, there was much more to the man I thought I knew. As a child, not even in my teens, I was bewildered and asked an uncle why grandpa was being saluted. My uncle's response stopped me in my tracks; **"Son, your grandfather is a hero."** Over the next several minutes, I learned how lucky I was to be loved and mentored by the man I simply called "Grandpa."

I learned he had fought in the battle for the Philippines, survived the infamous Bataan Death March, and endured 3 ½ years as a prisoner of war (POW). When the atomic bomb was dropped on Hiroshima, he was just 50 miles away at POW Camp Roku Rushi. Following his return to the United States, he served in various positions, became an Army Ranger, deployed to Vietnam, became an Army Aviator, and served at U.S. Embassies in Iran and Austria. He served his country for 32 years, made life-long friends, was happily married, and he loved life. He lived a life of significance by impacting several lives.

At the young age of 12, I found my purpose. I wanted to be like grandpa!

Finding Purpose

Several years after helping me find my purpose, grandpa passed away and was buried in Arlington, Virginia. The following year, the U.S. Army named the Fort Rucker Army Safety Center after him where his name is immortalized on the Conrad Safety Complex.

I aspired to follow in his footsteps by wanting to serve my country and become a person of character just like him. I became a United States Marine and served our nation for 30 years. During my retirement ceremony, I proudly wore my grandfather's Colonel rank insignia as a tribute to the man who had

61

profoundly influenced my life. He passed away in September 1992, just two weeks after I was commissioned a Second Lieutenant into the Marine Corps. He knew his legacy of service would continue, which brought me great comfort.

I exist because he endured. Anyone alive today has so many ancestors before us to thank. We are fortunate to be alive. It truly is a gift and I often wonder and hope that I am making my ancestors proud with the gift of life they made possible. It is most fitting that my retirement officer was my Uncle John, grandpa's third son. John was the first Marine I ever met and has been a mentor and role model my entire life. He has helped me through the most difficult times and shared my greatest joys. So, in many ways, my grandfather's mentorship has remained long after him.

5. **Who has influenced your life or helped you discover your purpose?**

_____

_____

_____

_____

_____

_____

_____

_____

The Republic of Texas

Living in Texas during my teenage years also had a positive impact on shaping my character. The Texas spirit of resilience, fearlessness, and an unwavering willingness to fight against all odds for something you believe in left a lasting impression on me. The Alamo, a symbol of Texas heritage, represents the unique culture and values of the state. In fact, you really cannot call yourself a Texan until you have visited the Alamo which is the embodiment of the State's culture. My first visit to the Alamo taught me that being a Texan is special. I was proud to be part of a culture built by names like Sam Houston, James Bowie, William Travis, Steven F. Austin, the Texas Rangers, and even Davy Crockett. Texas culture is a willingness to serve something greater than yourself with a spirit that is not afraid. These experiences nurtured my sense of determination and instilled the belief that no challenge is insurmountable while serving a worthy cause.

Attending Pine Tree High School in Longview, Texas was a wonderful experience. I was heavily involved in sports and multiple clubs and was fortunate to be surrounded by good people. During my freshman year, I competed in what was known as the National History Fair whose theme in 1985 was "triumphs and tragedies." My mom and I immediately thought of grandpa and came up with the idea of the Bataan Death

March as a story that was both a tragedy (the event) and a triumph (the human spirit). I was too young to realize the significance of the first-hand accounts and stories shared by all my grandfather's friends, all of whom were fellow prisoners of war. Some of the artifacts they shared with me included diaries, old photos, and never-before published accounts of their wartime experiences. One of the former POWs even gave me an autographed photo of General Douglas MacArthur presented to him when he later served as the General's aide-de-camp during the Korean War. Each of them had a letter from President Truman upon their repatriation to the United States following their time in captivity.

I was greatly honored to inform grandpa and his friends that I had won first place in the State of Texas. The stories I learned from these heroes only strengthened my purpose and resolve to serve my country in uniform. My pursuit to earn an appointment to the United States Military Academy created a thirst for knowledge and growth that could not be quenched. As such, I became involved in everything possible from the Debate team to Football, Track, Fellowship of Christian Athletes, the Drama Club, and Student Council. Although I obtained a prep school appointment, my passion to become a United States Marine and attend Auburn University resulting from a family trip to the Cotton Bowl was too great.

The Cotton Bowl and Auburn University

In 1986, at the age of 15, I had the privilege to attend the Cotton Bowl in Texas with my parents, both Auburn University alumni. The game pitted Auburn against Texas A&M, and the atmosphere was electrifying. I vividly recall the bustling streets, alive with the sound of enthusiastic fans, the rhythmic beat of drums, and the captivating performance by the band, majorettes, and flag line. I remember my parents' excitement in the moment and saying, "Son, trust us, you want to go to Auburn." Inside the stadium, I witnessed Bo Jackson make an incredible 74-yard run while the crowd went wild. I was hooked! The trip to the Cotton Bowl left an indelible impression and despite Auburn's loss in that game, my resolve was unwavering—I had made up my mind. I was going to Auburn University.

At the age of 15, I wanted to become a part of what I had just witnessed, the Auburn family! Three years later, I vividly recall leaving my home in Texas and my father dropping me off at an apartment complex I had never seen and with a handshake, he simply said, "Good luck son." A few days later, I met my roommate who would be sharing our small one-bedroom apartment. Having very little money and no acquaintances teaches you something about yourself, resilience. Fortunately, I met dozens of incredible people who were in the Naval ROTC program, on the Varsity Track team (I was a walk-on Pole Vaulter for two years under the legendary coach Mel Rosen), and some very good neighbors. Although not fully realizing the impactful words of the Auburn Creed, I began to embody the beliefs and values until they became a part of my character (hard work, human touch, a spirit that is not afraid).

At the completion of my Freshman Year, I bought a bus ticket to Dallas, Texas, closed my checking account which made the teller laugh and happily announce I only had 97 cents. My Uncle John found me a high-paying summer job loading air freight until the time came for me to fly to San Diego Naval Air Station where I was assigned to the Fast Frigate, the USS Stein for my Midshipman 4th Class "cruise." During my one month "deployment," I learned that humility, kindness, confidence, courage, a thirst for knowledge, and a commitment to excellence were paramount to a successful "cruise." All Midshipman were berthed with the enlisted Sailors for the duration of our short time on board. I absolutely loved the opportunity to learn from the experts while gaining valuable insights to why young men choose to serve our Country. In one word, I was inspired. My second Summer "deployment" was very similar, and my third summer was spent at the iconic United States Marine Corps Officer's Candidates School in Quantico, Virginia, "The Crossroads of the Marine Corps." Not for the faint of heart, I found OCS to be enjoyable because I knew to achieve my purpose, I had to succeed. As Frederick

Nietzsche once stated, "People will endure almost any How, to achieve their Why." [3] The training program at Auburn University was exceptional and all of us "Marine Option" Midshipmen were well prepared and completed OCS with ease.

    Auburn University laid the groundwork for my values, my character, and my future professional endeavors. Auburn's culture and legacy is something that must be seen and experienced, but once you do, those feelings remain with you forever. 37 years have passed since that cotton bowl experience. I spent four wonderful years attending Auburn, earning a degree in Business Management; I was a member of the NROTC and Varsity Track team, I met an Auburn girl who has been my bride for over 30 years. During three decades of service to my country as a Marine, Auburn has always been my anchor, my home. Regardless of where I found myself in the world, I was always greeted with a "War Eagle" from random members of the Auburn family whom I had never met. Just like becoming a United Staes Marine, becoming a member of the Auburn family is for life.

    In July 2022, just 10 weeks after my retirement ceremony, I had the immense honor of joining Auburn University on a full-time basis, assuming the role of Director for Human Resource Development and teaching leadership classes at the esteemed Harbert College of Business. I have found a new purpose back on the plains of Auburn where my foundation was built so many years ago. I am still serving what is most important to me, which is people, helping others achieve their full potential. My family made Auburn our permanent home in 2018 and we have no desire to ever move again. My wife reminds me that 17 military moves is enough to last a lifetime and we know how special Auburn is after having lived in six States and overseas. No place even comes close, and the heart and soul of this city is Auburn University. Michele is back to serving her purpose as a pharmacist for two family-owned pharmacies; my youngest daughter is thriving at Auburn High School; my oldest daughter is now in her sophomore year at Auburn University writing her own story and making her own memories, but those memories are united by the common bond that is defined as the Auburn Family.

Full Circle

"No man ever steps in the same river twice, for it's not the same river and he is not the same man." – Heraclitus

Reflecting upon my journey, I am struck by the remarkable transformation from the 12-year-old in awe of my grandfather, Colonel Eugene Conrad, to the 15-year-old kid who witnessed those unforgettable moments at the Cotton Bowl while growing up in Texas, to attending Auburn University, to serving my Country as a United States Marine, to the person I am today. It is astonishing to ponder how my 15-

year-old mind would have processed a vision 37 years later with me proudly wearing my grandfather's Colonel rank insignia as I retired at the same rank he had achieved. Equally remarkable is the fact that I currently have a daughter that is a beautiful Tiger Eye just like the ones marching in front of me at the Cotton Bowl so many years ago. And the best of all is celebrating over 30 years of marriage to my lovely wife and best friend who is the epitome of an Auburn girl. Also surreal is watching my youngest daughter perform (yes, she is also on the flag line) on the same High School football field that my wife did 37 years ago.

Life is Good!

Now it is your turn to reflect on your life's journey and who or what helped you find your purpose.

6. What events or people inspired you to become the person you are or hope to be?

Finding your purpose is a profound journey that evolves through encounters with people and experiences that shape our desires and goals in life. Reflecting on my grandfather's influence, the Texas spirit, the foundation built at Auburn University, the opportunity to serve my Country, each chapter has contributed to my growth and renewed sense of purpose. I hope you are inspired to reflect on your own purpose, for it is in finding our purpose that we truly come alive and lead with authenticity. Do not ever become upset over not being something; rather, look into yourself and find your story to understand who you are and who you are meant to be. As we conclude this chapter and reflect on Mark Twain's' opening quote…

7. **Have you discovered your purpose? If so, what is it?**

_____
_____
_____
_____
_____
_____
_____
_____
_____
_____

Notes:

1. Tom Brokaw, *The Greatest Generation*. Random House. 2001. Brokaw coined the term "The Greatest Generation" to describe the American men and women who served during World War II, both in uniform overseas and on the home front. Military victory required an All-in mindset by every United States citizen.
2. George Petrie. 1943. Also produced in the book, *Auburn Man, The Life and Times of George Petrie*, by Mike Jernigan. The Donnell Group, Montgomery, AL. 2007.
3. Steve Taylor. A Transformation of Purpose: From Selfishness to Altruism. Psychology Today. February 9, 2023.
https://www.psychologytoday.com/

Finding Your Story

Marines earning their Eagle, Globe, and Anchor [1]

Chapter Three

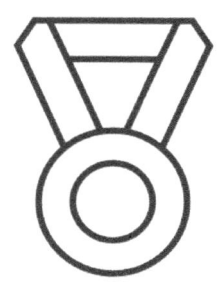

Finding Your Story

"Knowing yourself is the beginning of all wisdom."
                                                    -Aristotle

Over 2,000 years ago, Socrates heralded a stoic philosophy of deep reflection and to ask the simple question, why? Socrates stated "The highest form of human excellence is to question oneself…" [2]. I am certainly no philosopher; however, just like Socrates, *The Invisible Medal* will hopefully stimulate critical thinking and self-reflection. Socrates never claimed to be a teacher, he simply challenged individuals to engage in contemplation, ultimately leading them to their own insights. Instructors at the Air War College are encouraged to adopt the Socratic method of teaching their seminars comprised of twelve senior officers. The goal is not to teach them what to think, but why they think as they do, and to explain their thought process. In some respects, today's leadership coaches follow the Socratic method by asking multiple questions to reveal a treasure trove of internal awareness and understanding. Socrates may very well have been the world's first leadership coach. In keeping with this timeless wisdom,

> **I invite the reader to swim to the depths of their inner core where values, beliefs, assumptions, motivation, and bias reside.**

This is where you will find your authentic self. Then, true reflection can occur. When asked what they wished they had spent more time doing, nearly every retired General officer who spoke at the Air War College stated, "**I wish I spent more time reflecting.**" [3].

The fast-paced nature of life, the multitude of tasks and decisions, often leaves little room for introspection. Consider this: the adult mind makes approximately 35,000 decisions each day; 227 decisions solely related to food. [4]. For some like me, I am sure food decisions exceed 1,000, nonetheless, this realization underscores the significance of pausing to process the decisions we make or meditating in the morning or evening to reflect on the day's events and decisions yet to be made. Our world is full of a never-ending barrage of information. Social media, 24/7 news cycles, a constantly growing e-mail inbox both at work and at home, chores, phone calls, the list is endless. I find that trying to disconnect from the chaos is therapy for mind, body, and soul. In fact, I do my best thinking and problem-solving when I am not focused on thinking. Finding a quiet place, walking in nature, attending a church service, staring at the vast ocean are ways to find my center. Sounds impossible, right? Who has the time to do nothing?

Consider President Ronald Reagan, likely one of the busiest people alive while he was in office during the years of Mutually Assured Destruction and constant threat of nuclear war. Despite his work calendar, he always made the time to write in a diary. He paused to reflect and to process, so he could more effectively lead the free world. Today, his diaries are on display at the Ronald Reagan Museum in Simi Valley, California and stand as a testament to the value of self-reflection and how self-reflection is indeed an art for the most effective leaders.

Delving into the depths of our thoughts is essential to bring out the greatness within.

As we progress through the following chapters, I encourage you to actively participate by writing down your thoughts.

Storytelling

Patti Digh reminded us of the importance of stories when she said, "the shortest distance between two people is a story." [5]. All of us have unique life experiences. We grow from those events and long to tell others what we have learned so they can either share in our joy or avoid our pain. According to James Kerr,

> Stories are the way we understand life and our place in it. Stories teach children the difference between right and wrong, good, and bad, loyalty and love. Once we are adults, stories help us understand who we are, what we want, want we stand for, what we stand against, and why we do things. [6]

The best stories choose the right words. Words are powerful. When chosen wisely, words can invoke images and feelings that will touch a person's heart. Words can lead a hardened Soldier to tears. Words can lead a docile person to anger. Words can inspire a person to action. Consider the images and feelings that are aroused by simply hearing, "I have a dream," or "We will never surrender."

Martin Luther King's famous speech was delivered to over 250,000 people in front of the Lincoln Memorial. It has been noted that toward the end of his speech, he departed from his prepared comments to describe his dream, which became a rallying cry for our nation. [7] I am emotionally touched every time I hear his "I have a dream" speech.

In the "darkest hour" of World War II when the fall of France was imminent and the fate of Great Britain seemed all but lost, the British Prime Minister, Winston Churchill delivered a moving speech to the House of Commons which captured the heart of every British citizen revealing their grit and determination. Politicians, military servicemen, and civilians became united in their resolve to continue the struggle and to "never surrender."

When someone is gifted with the ability to translate a personal experience into words and share their experience with others in an inspirational way, the ingredients for touching and changing lives emerge. The ability to deliver a message that connects with human beings in such a way that it inspires them is beyond powerful; it is life changing. In my youth, I watched an old recording of General Douglas MacArthur's farewell address to the corps of cadets at West Point. General MacArthur spoke of a serviceman's essence characterized by Duty, Honor, and Country. Those words resonated with me so much that it set me on a path of discovery to learn from my grandfathers and uncles who served our nation. Their stories and General MacArthur's words inspired me to serve my nation.

Storytelling does not need to be long to be significant. Consider President Abraham Lincoln's Gettysburg address. Less than 275 words in length, Lincoln's three-minute-long talk defined the significance of the Civil War less than five months after the Battle of Gettysburg. Surprisingly, President Lincoln's talk followed the primary speaker, Edward Everett who spoke for two hours. However, it is Lincoln's short speech, which touched everyone's heartstrings and continues to do so today.

So, what is your story?

8. Tell me about yourself (i.e. your elevator speech)?

My elevator speech is:

> Hi, my name is Chris. I have recently returned to Auburn having completed 30 years' service in the Marine Corps. During my time in uniform, I was fortunate to work with incredible people, travel the world, and acquire life-long values and leadership skills. Some of those include humility, integrity, teamwork, loyalty, problem-solving, and helping people achieve their full potential. The Auburn creed has been a strong part of my beliefs, and I would love any opportunity to give back and serve the institution I love. Please keep me in mind if you hear of any open positions. War Eagle!

The above "elevator speech" was developed in 2019 during the military Transition Readiness course. Although I was never in a situation where I needed to recite the speech, taking the time to think about what I wanted to say if given 30 seconds to make an impression on a potential employer was extremely helpful. During an interview for my current role, I was able to include portions of my "elevator speech" in response to multiple questions I was asked. Everyone possesses a unique narrative. What drove them to their chosen profession? Do they have a higher purpose that fuels their passions, perhaps a yearning for belonging, or simply to serve a cause greater than themselves.

Have you unraveled the depths of your personal "Why"? As Simon Sinek famously captured, our "Why" encompasses our purpose in life. [8] It is possible that you are already living it, even if you are unaware. Can you articulate your "why" as a story? Author Steven Spatz so aptly states "Storytelling is the best medium of communication. The best leaders articulate who they are and what's important to them through stories." [9]. I was relatively well established on my personal leadership journey when I discovered my true "Why" which is simply: **To Help Others Achieve Their Full Potential.**

Crucibles

There is a powerful event that takes place at the completion of Marine Corps bootcamp which marks the final step in transforming our young Americans into a United States Marine. It is called **The Crucible** and takes place at the culmination of an intense 13-week boot camp. The Crucible is a grueling four and a half days of combat-like scenarios, minimal sleep, and high-stress situations.

Marines who have experienced The Crucible will recall the camaraderie among their teammates and desire to perform to the best of their ability. Despite their bodies being so tired, they can barely move, their excitement as The Crucible enters the final day is just enough to keep them moving, especially when cadences are belted out for the last half-mile of a grueling hike on the final day. At its completion, a life-changing moment awaits the recruits as they crest a hill to witness the sight of the American flag and the Marine Corps flag, alongside their drill instructors. No longer addressed as recruits, they are now recognized as United States Marines, bestowed with the symbolic eagle, globe, and anchor (EGA) thus signifying their entry into the revered brotherhood and sisterhood that is the Marine Corps. Although many hardened new Marines believe they can complete the ceremony without emotion, almost all succumb to the moment and their eyes "sweat" (Marines don't cry, but we are emotional beings, so our eyes will often "sweat"). [10]. This poignant ceremony resonates deeply with anyone who has experienced it firsthand and epitomizes the fact that **one does not simply join the Marine Corps; you become a United States Marine and will remain so your entire life**. The brotherhood, sisterhood, esprit-de-corps, and values of honor, courage, and commitment become a part of you. You are part of something special, a legacy like no other. Through boot camp and The Crucible, you have been changed for life.

The term "crucible" holds significant meaning outside the Marine Corps. In a 2002 Harvard Business Review article, esteemed authors researched crucibles of leadership, studying the responses of 60 senior leaders. The essence of a crucible lies in breaking something down to its fundamental elements.

Like the Marine Corps Crucible, individuals can undergo their own crucibles, enduring trials that test their character and resilience.

The remarkable insights of authors Warren Bennis and Robert Thomas tell us that exceptional leaders handle crucible moments by seeking meaning from their experiences as a mechanism for growth. [11]. Rather than succumbing to the bitter aspects of an event, they embrace the opportunity to learn and emerge stronger. In Proverbs 27:17, it is written "As iron sharpens iron, so one person sharpens another." [12]. Strong leaders will only become stronger and more resilient following crucible events.

Further research revealed that top business leaders who experienced intense and unexpected crucibles fundamentally transformed their **leadership philosophy.** A leadership philosophy reflects an individual's perspective on serving the needs of others and will guide their approach to leadership. It encapsulates personal values and wisdom derived from their crucibles to serve as a compass that enhances both our lives and the lives of those we are privileged to lead. By embracing crucibles and their lessons, leaders gain invaluable insights and a profound understanding of how to grow through adversity.

Crucibles are a potent force, capable of shaping ordinary people into extraordinary leaders.

It is through these transformative crucibles that leaders discover the true extent of their capabilities, uncover hidden reservoirs of resilience, and forge a profound connection with the purpose and meaning behind their leadership journey. I have experienced many crucibles throughout my life. One such crucible occurred in 2006 while I was assigned as a department head at Marine Aviation Weapons and Tactics Squadron-1 in Yuma, Arizona. As our arduous six-week training exercise ended, some of our Marines developed a well-thought-out plan to return communications equipment to a Marine Corps base three hours away. They wanted the Marines tasked with this duty to return in time for our closing ceremony and to travel home with their unit. The only problem was their plan required an extremely early departure of 3am. Although the plan mitigated all safety concerns with all potential issues addressed, something did not sit well with me. My gut told me so. Nonetheless, after multiple discussions, I gave in and approved the plan. Around 4am, I was awakened by a phone call informing me the Marines had been involved in a head-on collision. Thankfully, the Marines and other drivers were okay; however, damage to our equipment and vehicles was irreparable. My lesson through this crucible was clear; never violate your gut instinct!

9. Have you experienced any life crucibles?

What were they and what did you learn about yourself?

___
___
___
___
___
___
___
___
___
___
___
___
___
___
___
___
___
___
___

Notes

1. Dan Doyle. "Here's Why The End Of USMC Boot Camp Is Called 'The Crucible.' https://blog.theveteranssite.greatergood.com/usmc-crucible/. The photo comes from a video capture in Dan Doyle's article which references YOUTUBE/WGN RADIO VIDEO.
2. Socrates. https://www.goodreads.com/quotes/499120-i-know-you-won-t-believe-me-but-the-highest-form.
3. Throughout each academic year, senior-ranking officials address the entire class at the Air War College with a focus on leadership.
4. Jennifer Gutmann. Decision-Making: One of Our Greatest Challenges Today. A blueprint of exercises to help you make better decisions at home and at work. Psychology Today. www.psychologytoday.com. Posted February 17, 2022.
5. Patti Digh. https://www.goodreads.com/quotes/825629-the-shortest-distance-between-two-people-is-a-story.
6. James Kerr. Legacy, What the All Blacks Can Teach us about the Business of Life. Constable, London, England. 2013.
7. Carmine Gallo. "How Martin Luther King Improvised 'I Have A Dream'." Forbes Magazine. August 2013.
8. Simon Sinek. *Start with Why: How Great Leaders Inspire Everyone to Take Action.* (New York: Penguin, 2009).
9. Steven Spatz. The 1 leadership skill everybody overlooks. www.theladders.com. December 15, 2018.
10. Reflections shared by Marine Sergeant Bryan Tutton in Auburn on October 13th 2023.
11. Warren Bennis and Robert Thomas, Crucibles of Leadership. Harvard Business Review. September 2002.
12. Bible, New International Version. Proverbs 27:17.

A Leadership Philosophy

Photo of author during a staff meeting, 2002

Chapter Four

A Leadership Philosophy

"The most important journey is the one inward."
- Shannon L. Alder

One of my first leadership crucibles as a young professional occurred in 1997 when I was the commander for a long-range radar platoon in Beaufort, South Carolina. Having spent three years in Beaufort, I was only a few months away from my first military Permanent Change of Station (PCS) move to Fort McPherson, Georgia.

Our Squadron's focus was preparing for combat scenarios through rigorous training. It was well before 9/11 with the Global War on Terrorism still several years away, so whenever an opportunity arose for a "real-world" operation, we were all eager to participate. That is precisely what happened when our organization received a deployment order for counter-drug operations in South America. Everyone wanted to be part of it, but due to personnel restrictions, we could only send two platoons out of the three in our company.

Inevitably, we faced a tough decision which led us to carefully select the best Marines to form the two platoons required for deployment thereby leaving behind those who were about to PCS (like me), were injured, or considered less qualified. It was a challenging situation, but our mission's success was paramount. To compound matters, approximately one week after the two platoons had departed, our squadron received news from headquarters Marine Corps that we would undergo a combat readiness evaluation. This evaluation, with only two weeks' notice, was a grueling test that could result in the commanding officer being fired on the spot if the unit failed.

My commanding officer, Lieutenant Colonel Brian Dingess was a leader we all admired and respected—a patient, kind, and humble person who enabled us to succeed both personally and professionally. He epitomized what everybody would want to have in a leader, and we were determined not to let him down.

Upon receipt of the pending evaluation, Lieutenant Colonel Dingess called me into his office and expressed his concerns. With everyone deployed, we only had one platoon left, and they would be the ones evaluated, ultimately determining if he would keep his position as Commanding Officer. In response, I assured him that we would do our best. That is when I met the newly formed "remain behind" platoon. In that moment, it felt like we had created a land of misfit toys from the Christmas classic, *Rudolph the Red-Nosed Reindeer*, where many felt they were unwanted. [1] It was truly a shame because every Marine in our unit was exceptional. They just had not made the cut for the "A" or "B" team for deployment. "You are a misfit" was the unfortunate message we unintentionally conveyed; however, I knew deep down that their self-perception could not be further from the truth. I learned a timeless lesson:

> **Every member of your team wants and needs to feel valued. Treat everyone as if they are important and vital members of the team because they are.**

It is so important for leaders to uplift every member of our team regardless of position, title, or proficiency. This team was more like the *Avengers*, a group of extraordinary individuals with untapped potential. We had two weeks to prove ourselves. Sensing their initial hesitation, I was determined to change their mindset. We came together as a united team, driven by a shared goal not only to pass the combat readiness evaluation but to excel and prove to everyone that we were indeed "good enough."

The grueling evaluation came and departed. Our "misfit island" platoon had not only passed, but they also achieved the best score our Squadron had ever received, a 98%. This experience taught me that every human being possesses the capacity to be extraordinary. Everyone can be a high performing, high potential employee. When we invest in helping individuals unlock their full potential, the collective power of the team is unstoppable. And that's exactly what they did.

The events which unfolded during my last few weeks in Beaufort, SC remained dormant in my memory until three years later. I had moved to Fort MacPherson, Georgia where I had a wonderful three years before moving to Quantico, Virginia for a one-year resident Command and Control Systems Course (CCSC). While attending CCSC in 2000, I read a troubling Department of Defense (DoD) exit survey that identified the top four reasons why service members had left military service. Those reasons were:

1. Lack of confidence in leaders
2. Lack of job challenge
3. Lack of responsibility
4. Lack of recognition

The cited reasons identified by the DoD exit survey made me angry with the feeling that military leaders were failing those who volunteered to serve our great Nation. I was called to do something about it, so I took pen to paper and began to write. As I began to write, my mind reflected on the experience in Beaufort, SC where Marines had excelled despite their perceived inability to do so. The more I reflected on how our team of "misfits" achieved near perfect results, my leadership philosophy materialized--**T-E-A-M**. Leaders who continuously **train**, **empower**, **acknowledge**, and **mentor** their employees exhibit an understanding of leading with a higher purpose. Even though the T-E-A-M concept as a leadership philosophy had not fully materialized in 1997, the essence was present in our actions as we prepared for the pending evaluation. We instinctively understood that nurturing and empowering each team member was vital to unleash their potential.

Interestingly, in 2022, McKinsey released a similar exit survey so troubling that it ushered in the popular phrase, "The Great Resignation." [2] Recognizing the importance of training, empowering, acknowledging, and mentoring can help mitigate the reasons why people leave and foster a thriving and loyal team. It is an undeniable reality that many people are leaving their jobs in large numbers. The top four reasons cited in 2022 are eerily like the DoD report 22 years earlier. The McKinsey study concluded that the top reasons for this phenomenon are:

    1. Lack of career development opportunities

    2. Inadequate compensation

3. Uncaring and uninspiring leaders
4. Lack of meaningful work

Not every leader has the charisma of Martin Luther King Jr., the vision of Walt Disney, the resolve of Winston Churchill, or the humility of Nelson Mandela. However, anyone can apply leadership principles to enable those we are privileged to lead. Leaders who study the reasons why people leave their jobs, and institute basic leadership principles can significantly reduce the voluntary early departure of our employees.

A leader blessed with natural charisma can motivate their employees, but the rest of us can be equally effective through training, empowering, acknowledging, and mentoring our team. I learned the value of the T-E-A-M philosophy in 1997 when we were given two weeks to prepare a junior crew of Marines for a major exercise and combat evaluation. Furthermore, application of the T-E-A-M philosophy can address many of the concerns that create disillusionment among people in today's workforce. [3]

Train

Today's leaders must foster a climate of continuous training and professional development. In an environment where responsibilities have been increasing while the numbers of personnel have been decreasing, many leaders have grown reluctant to send their employees on temporary assigned duty for training. Too often, a boss will rationalize their actions by saying that the individual is far too valuable to our organization to be gone for any period. I will admit it seems counter-intuitive for high performing teams to choose to be without their top performers. Productivity might go down when your best people are away for extended periods to attend professional development or training. I remember one of my previous commanders tell me, "Chris, if it doesn't hurt when you send somebody off to do training, then you're sending the wrong person."

Despite their value to the organization, employees will become disillusioned if not given professional development opportunities. Restricting opportunities for professional development leads to employee's lack of job challenge and lack of career development, two reasons cited in the DoD and McKinsey reports.

Sending employees to training events a few times a year will not address their concerns; however, implementing a culture of continuous training and development will create the environment employees desire. Leaders must foster a climate of constant learning to promote the level of growth and job satisfaction necessary to retain our greatest asset, people. The welcome side effects of Training will be increased proficiency, knowledge, confidence, morale, and challenge. The fourth most cited reason for service members leaving the military in 2000 was that their jobs were not challenging enough. The 2022 McKinsey report cited lack of career development as the number one reason employees were leaving their job. If leaders take the time to train employees, then hold them accountable for new tasks and responsibilities, the result will be an added challenge along with career development and advancement.

When leaders encourage professional growth, job satisfaction increases, which motivates employees to remain. Conversely, failure to train employees can result in terrible consequences such as their inability to accomplish what is expected of them. Employees cannot be challenged or given greater responsibilities until properly trained.

We applied the training aspect of the T-E-A-M philosophy in preparation for the evaluation in 1997 by building a training guide with a test on each function the Marines were to perform during the evaluation. A computer program was also built to simulate the exercise, which our platoon completed several times. At first, we stumbled and failed repeatedly in both the simulation and written tests; however, with each attempt, we learned valuable lessons and grew more proficient. Our increased competence instilled a sense of confidence that propelled us forward and achieve maximum potential. Hard training became a foundational pillar of our success. Not only did this challenge the Marines, but everyone agreed that the simulation and training guide were major factors in our ultimate success in achieving a near-perfect grade. Leaders must ensure that training is useful, relevant, and applicable to an employee's growth and job proficiency. If leaders take the time to allow for training and development, our employees will respond to the challenge. They will be empowered to act.

Empower

Empowerment means giving official authority to others. Through empowerment, leaders reveal trust in their employees. Trusting someone's judgment will have an enormous impact on their desire to prove the leader correct. In other words,

Giving trust creates a desire to earn trust.

An employee will not grow until given responsibilities greater than those required by their current position. For example, if a leader treats a Sergeant like a Sergeant, that is likely all he will ever be. However, if the leader empowers the Sergeant with the responsibilities of a Staff Sergeant, then that is what they will strive to become. Many junior Marines agree. In an article in the Marine Corps Gazette, Corporal Zachary Martin writes that "failure to give responsibility to NCOs [non-commissioned officers] produces NCOs who are indeed unworthy of responsibility." [4] The same is true for any industry, including higher learning institutions like Auburn University. Giving employees additional responsibilities will help them grow into positions of higher responsibility such as Director, Supervisor, or even associate vice president. Empowering new responsibilities can be something like giving an employee responsibility to manage your unit's budget.

The benefits of empowering others are immeasurable because empowerment enhances morale by increasing the individual's identity within a group. As a result, initiative and mutual trust will become second nature. People most likely come to work with an attitude of doing their job well; however, they will perform tasks and assignments with more enthusiasm and initiative for a leader who empowers them. Empowerment yields trust. Marine Corps Doctrinal Publication 6 (MCDP-6) discusses mutual trust as a cornerstone for cooperation:

> A senior trusts subordinates to carry out the assigned missions competently with minimal supervision.
>
> Subordinates meanwhile trust that the senior will provide the necessary guidance and will support them loyally and fully, even when they make mistakes. [6]

Trust must be earned by employees, but it also must be freely given by supervisors. When you empower someone, you build trust by giving them responsibility and allowing them to earn that trust. Leaders must give trust first and allow people to earn that trust. It is a paradigm shift for many leaders to first

A Leadership Philosophy

trust; however, the opposite can create a self-fulfilling prophecy by empowering individuals with trepidation and then micromanaging their every move, waiting to "catch them doing wrong". [7] True empowerment requires trust and allows individuals to achieve their potential, thereby providing purpose and value to their work. Leaders who empower their employees demonstrate their trust in them. Employees who enthusiastically take on new responsibilities make clear their belief and confidence in their leaders. Too many leaders are afraid to apply the simple principle of empowerment.

Empowering subordinates should not be feared but practiced regularly and is the best way to demonstrate trust and confidence in others.

Unfortunately, too many leaders want to keep power to themselves, disfranchising their employees in the process. Many leaders fear empowerment because they are afraid their employees will make mistakes. Consequently, leaders fail to delegate and thus create disillusioned personnel. Leaders who empower tentatively create a self-fulfilling prophecy. In other words, they expect the employee to fail, so they indeed, fail. The leaders have laid the groundwork for failure by undermining self-confidence.

The third most-cited reason for service members leaving the military in 2000 was that their leaders had failed to place them in positions of responsibility. The McKinsey report cited lack of meaningful work as the fourth most cited reason which led to the "Great Resignation." If employees are empowered, their job satisfaction increases, and they will find more meaning in their work. They have more responsibility, they are challenged, and they want to stay in the organization. Failure to empower may not result in a failure to accomplish a specific mission; however, leaders who stifle employee growth and initiative will also stifle their interest in continuing to work for the organization.

Empowerment is a superpower which transforms people and teams.

During the 1997 exercise, we decided to divide the platoon into three smaller sections. Since we lacked additional officers, we entrusted each platoon to a Sergeant, empowering them with the responsibility of a Lieutenant. Though they initially lacked confidence, I reassured them, saying they would accomplish our mission because they were knowledgeable, motivated, and outstanding leaders who I trusted without reservation. Their motivation soared, and they rose to the occasion, exceeding all expectations. When we empower others to achieve their full potential, magic happens. Through empowerment, these Sergeants met the challenge and handled themselves and their Marines with distinction.

Acknowledge

The fourth most cited reason why servicemembers left the military in 2000 was lack of recognition. Acknowledgment is such an important leadership skill which is missing in too many organizations. Acknowledging subordinates is not accomplished solely by awarding people with medals or certificates that usually are presented long after their contribution has been made. Instead, leaders should take time daily to shine the spotlight on others. Leaders should not assume that a good performance review or a job-family promotion given at the end of several months of dedication and effort will take care of this aspect of the T-E-A-M philosophy. Dr. Wes Roberts writes that leaders should "be generous with small tokens of appreciation; they will multiply in returned loyalty and service." [7] Good leaders acknowledge their employees continuously by thanking them for their work and contributions to the team. If someone falters or needs assistance, then good leaders will provide direction or find someone to help. Daily acknowledgment is about being visible, showing that you are right there alongside your teammates. It is small gestures like a pat on the back or asking someone about their weekend, their kids soccer game, or their part-time job that demonstrates acknowledgment. Leaders must recognize when people need a coach, a cheerleader, a teammate, or all the above, simultaneously. This can only happen if the leader takes the time to acknowledge and communicate with those they are entrusted to lead.

Most important, acknowledging others means that the leader must listen. The importance of leaders leaving their offices to make personal contact with their people cannot be overstated. More than ever in this post-COVID age of technology, leaders must make personal contact with their teams and employees. We cannot substitute e-mail and voicemail for leadership. Leaders who listen to their subordinates find out what their people are thinking and, oftentimes, learn better ways of doing things, while also learning what motivates members of their team. Leaders also must be humble enough to accept the reality of learning better ways to accomplish goals or objectives from their employees. Such communications with our employees demonstrate genuine care. The words of former President Teddy Roosevelt provide timeless advice.

> *People will not care how much you know, until they know how much you care.* [8]

This statement cuts to the heart of the third most cited reason in the 2022 McKinsey report as to why employees quit, "Uninspiring leaders." Teddy Roosevelt's simple, yet powerful truth underscores the essence of servant leadership. It emphasizes the fact that intelligence, experience, past achievements, and positions hold little significance if the leader fails to genuinely demonstrate care and support for their team. Building a successful team relies on cultivating an environment where people feel valued, respected, and nurtured. Therefore, as young leaders, it is essential to prioritize showing care and concern for our team members, rather than solely showcasing our own knowledge and expertise. During my time in the military, I often heard officers say, "when people stop coming to you for advice, that is when you have stopped being their leader."

Leadership is not telling people you are in charge; leadership is serving the needs of those under your charge.

In other words, before you can inspire your team to achieve their full potential, you must show them that you care. This is vital for anyone desiring to lead with a higher purpose and earn invisible medals. Understanding that everyone has a life beyond work, whether it involves their children's soccer games or other commitments, being present, engaged, and communicating is the best way to show people you care about them.

A striking anecdote involving President John F. Kennedy during the early stages of the race to the moon exemplifies the significance of recognizing every individual's contribution to a team. While visiting NASA, President Kennedy inadvertently encountered a janitor. Rather than ignoring him, the President engaged in a conversation, expressing curiosity about their responsibilities. The janitor, without hesitation, responded, "Well, Mr. President, I'm a member of the team that's going to put the first man on the moon." [9] This interaction highlights the profound understanding NASA had fostered—a recognition that every person, regardless of their position—plays a crucial role in achieving mission success.

NASA's success story serves as a testament to the importance of embracing a holistic perspective on teamwork. By acknowledging the intrinsic value of every individual and ensuring that no one is overlooked, teams can function cohesively and achieve remarkable outcomes. The realization that each person contributes to the collective effort strengthens the bonds within the team and empowers individuals to commit to excellence.

The wisdom shared by President Roosevelt and the anecdote involving President Kennedy highlights essential aspects of leadership. Genuine care, support, and recognition of every team member's value are critical for building cohesive and successful teams. By embodying these principles, leaders create environments that foster growth, trust, and collaboration, which ultimately enables their teams to reach unparalleled achievement.

Lack of recognition can be easily rectified by leaders who simply acknowledge and appreciate people for their contributions to the team. I vividly recall the impact my wife had on members of the U.S. Embassy team in Abu Dhabi. During my assignment as military liaison to the United Arab Emirates, Michele applied for and was selected to the prestigious role of Community Liaison Officer. She thrived in this role because she genuinely cared about people. Her compassion for others led to envisioning and implementing the first-ever International-Recognition Day for the Embassy. Several Embassy employees were from many different countries, so the International Day Michele organized encouraged our international teammates to showcase their culture. Everyone fully embraced the opportunity, dressing in their nation's clothing, sharing specialty food dishes, singing, and dancing. The entire day was full of appreciation, fun, and pride; however, what Michele truly achieved was **unity**. People were acknowledged in ways they had never been before, leading to a much stronger Embassy team. During our family's farewell, an Embassy teammate remarked, "the receiving line for Michele was longer than the one for our previous Ambassador." Such a wonderful comment for Michele who simply chose to acknowledge others and earned an Invisible Medal.

We do not need implement something as elaborate as an International Day to acknowledge others. Simply taking the time to say "thank you" is a powerful way to show others that they are valued. It costs nothing, yet it boosts morale, increases self-worth, and reinforces the sense of purpose within the team. I encourage every leader to try it. Walk through your organization and sincerely thank people for what they're doing. In fact, we should do this for everyone, store clerks, restaurant workers, police officers, teachers, etc. It is easy to do, and it is free. But it shows people that they are appreciated. After a recent keynote discussing this concept, a participant came to me afterwords and enthusiastically shook my hand and said it best, "**everybody is somebody.**" We all have value. Every single human being in an organization has extreme value for the overall success of your team. Besides, acknowledging someone not only increases their feelings of self-worth, but will also put a smile on their face. You may even earn an invisible medal.

Leaders who fail to engage or acknowledge their subordinates set up a devastating cycle of failure. James Kouzes makes the following observation in a book about the challenge of leadership: "People repeat behavior that is rewarded, avoid behavior that is punished, and drop or forget behavior that produces neither result." [10] If leaders take the time to listen to and acknowledge their people, employees will have increased feelings of self-worth and their individual value to the organization. Furthermore, when formally recognized for excellence, employees learn to appreciate the value that their leaders place on hard work and learn to connect effort and sacrifice with recognition. Once an employee has reached a level of self-actualization and knows their efforts will be appreciated, they will be motivated to remain with the organization.

I applied the acknowledge aspect of the T-E-A-M philosophy during the 1997 evaluation by approaching Marines individually and acknowledging the work they were doing. Immediately following the exercise, those who performed exceptionally well were awarded medals, meritorious masts, or recognition in front of the detachment. I found that those who were recognized did not become complacent but worked even more diligently after the exercise, while those not recognized set a goal to earn awards and future recognition. Regardless, everyone felt appreciated and valued and knew that without their direct contribution, the entire team would have failed.

Mentor

The number one reason people left the military in 2000 was the lack of confidence in their leaders. I was shocked reading the DoD exit survey; however, I understood all too well because of my early experiences as a young Lieutenant. My first Squadron had adopted a short-lived Marine Corps Mentorship program. Our Squadron's few Captains were told to select one of our many Lieutenants to "mentor." No one selected me. I remember feeling rejected and thinking, shouldn't everyone have a mentor? Can the mentors themselves not learn from those being mentored? Everyone has potential and everyone should be mentored. All should share thoughts, ideas, and experiences regardless of position or title. This not only unleashes potential within individuals but also potential for your entire team. To be blunt, I was left incredibly disillusioned and made a point at that moment to treat my future teams differently. Everyone would be mentored.

Mentoring is the final element of the T-E-A-M philosophy and—just as the other T-E-A-M leadership traits—should be practiced continuously. Dictionaries define mentor as a "trusted counselor or guide." Some believe mentoring is an art that cannot be formalized, while others believe mentoring is a science that should be formalized. Both are correct. Formal programs demonstrate an organization's commitment to development, growth, and succession planning. However, informal mentorship is the real glue that binds the strongest teams. Mentoring can simply be taking the time to express a personal or professional experience to someone to enhance job performance or personal growth. Mentoring is not only top-down and bottom-up, but also side-to-side and should be open and continuous for all.

In fact, mentorship is so important, it can mitigate all the top four reasons cited in "The Great Resignation" of 2022. Obviously, to inspire confidence, leaders must be proficient in their jobs, but to inspire the confidence that leads to retention leaders must take the time to mentor and be mentored. The result is an implied message that the leader values others. Leaders who mentor demonstrate genuine interest in and an appreciation for their employees. Mentoring builds trust and mutual respect. When leaders encourage an atmosphere of constant mentoring, their teammates will develop feelings of self-worth and a sense of belonging. I have gained enormous confidence in and respect for the leaders who have taken the time to mentor me.

Not mentoring or adhering solely to strict mentor-protege relationships isolates those individuals without an assigned mentor. Every single person in an organization should be a protege, not just a select few, as a formalized program creates. Furthermore, if mentoring is not encouraged, then the underlying message is that the leader does not really care about the growth and development of their employees.

Mentorship is a fundamental cultural aspect of top-performing organizations and should not solely be viewed as top-down guidance but extends to bottom-up, and peer-to-peer interactions. Each person possesses unique strengths and skills, and the ability to mentor others within the organization fosters growth. Mentorship extends beyond job-related matters; it encompasses life pillars (chapter one). There may be areas outside our professional lives that we are curious about or desire to learn more from, and there are always individuals who can serve as mentors. By fostering open communication and breaking down barriers, mentorship becomes a catalyst for personal and professional growth. We should all embrace the role of being both mentor and mentee, sharing our knowledge and experiences to uplift others, while simultaneously learning from our teammates.

Mentoring can be specific, general, immediate, or long term and really boils down to this: If someone has experience or unique knowledge, then that knowledge should be shared with everyone, regardless of rank or position. The primary benefit of mentoring is the open lines of communication that will be fostered within an organization. Sir Isaac Newton had this to say when asked how it was that he knew so much: "The reason I see as far as I do is because I stand upon the shoulders of giants."[11] When experiences are shared, learning grows exponentially, and we all "can see the future."

When leaders encourage mentorship in their organizations, they informally introduce the value of humility and trust where people feel comfortable admitting what they do not know. An environment is created where learning and growth are embraced. By mentoring and being mentored, communication, trust, vulnerability, and a sense of belonging flourish within the team. It takes time, but when you walk around your organization and observe people talking about their weekend or something that they've learned or trying to teach somebody not just a job skill, but a life skill, you will know you have achieved the right climate of teamwork through mentorship.

During the exercise in 1997, we encouraged an open exchange of mentorship. I shared with the crew Sergeants management techniques I had learned, and the Gunnery Sergeant shared with me her experiences with preparation for an exercise evaluation. The Corporals taught me the technical aspects of their work, and I taught them the relevance of their tasks to the "bigger picture." The bottom line is that we were all taking time to mentor one another, and as a result, we accomplished great things. Professional business publications identify the power of mentoring: "In the heroic organizations, people mentor each other unselfishly." [12]

The T-E-A-M Leadership Philosophy Works

Good leaders strive to build and maintain effective teams. By following the T-E-A-M leadership philosophy, leaders can establish teams that will work together to accomplish missions and goals. Once team goals become more important than individual goals, the organization achieves maximum efficiency: "An organization operates most effectively when its members think of themselves as belonging to one or more groups characterized by high levels of loyalty, cooperation, morale and commitment to the group mission." [13] Through application of the T-E-A-M philosophy, individuals are recognized as people who are valued. Employees also value themselves because they have been inspired by their leaders.

T-E-A-M became my leadership philosophy in 2000 after deep reflection following one of my earliest leadership crucibles. Incorporating this philosophy into every leadership role I have held has taught me the universal values of the T-E-A-M philosophy. The T-E-A-M leadership philosophy helped mitigate the top reasons why people choose to leave their jobs, whether while I was on active duty or now as a Director at Auburn University. When we provide our team members with **training** and growth opportunities along with increased challenges, they will excel. **Empowerment** plays a vital role in fostering career development. By entrusting our team with additional responsibilities and allowing them to take ownership, we enable their growth. Compensation is not solely about money; it is also about making people feel valued and ensuring happiness in their roles. When we **acknowledge** our team members appropriately, we provide feelings of self-worth. **Mentorship** is essential in combating uncaring or uninspiring leadership. By dedicating time to mentor others, we demonstrate our commitment to their development, growth, and well-being.

All leaders, regardless of their charisma or natural abilities to lead, can enhance their effectiveness through the T-E-A-M leadership philosophy. I adhered to the T-E-A-M philosophy during a challenging leadership crucible in my career and found that the Marines became more committed to one another thereby achieving excellence. The T-E-A-M philosophy works. Supervisors who use it will grow as leaders while unleashing the full potential in their teams. They will also have the satisfaction of knowing that they contributed to the retention of the fine people we are privileged and entrusted to lead.

I encourage you to consider the T-E-A-M philosophy in your leadership approach. Ultimately, consistency of character and genuine care for our team members will enable winning teams; however, to truly lead with authenticity, I encourage you to develop your own leadership philosophy based on your personal crucibles and your values. If T-E-A-M works for you, fantastic; if not, develop your own philosophy and stick to it.

When we reflect upon our crucible moments and grow from those experiences, it becomes something that is unique to us. We can share the stories, but we have had an impact by learning from our leadership crucibles. Reflecting on our experiences and learning from them allows us to develop a personal leadership philosophy—a compass that guides us and how we care for others. It has been over two decades since I first developed the T-E-A-M leadership philosophy, and it sits on my desk even today as my accountability compass. These questions serve as the cornerstone of my leadership philosophy to ensure I remain true to what I believe as a leader. To ensure I truly uphold my core leadership philosophy of training, empowering, acknowledging, and mentoring?

> 1. Am I equipping and **training** my team to reach their full potential, not only in their professional lives but also in their personal lives?

> 2. Am I **empowering** my team members to take ownership and run with their responsibilities, or am I falling into the trap of micromanagement?

> 3. How many people did I genuinely **acknowledge** today? Did I focus on catching people doing things right rather than catching them doing things wrong?

> 4. Did I make time to **mentor** someone today, and equally important, did I remain open to being mentored by others?

As we grow and face new crucibles, we can refine our leadership philosophy. Our leadership journey never ends; it continuously evolves, and we encounter new crucibles along the way. In 2005, I had the opportunity to hear a keynote address

A Leadership Philosophy

from James Hunter who discussed his leadership concepts illustrated in his book, *The Servant*. The following year, I received an e-mail from the spouse of a Marine I previously served with (see chapter one). The contents of that e-mail and the knowledge I gained from James Hunter's talk transformed my perspective on leadership, and I was all-in on becoming a servant leader (**The Invisible Medal**). Adding the concept of servant leadership to the T-E-A-M philosophy, created **T-E-A-M-S**, and my modified compass for how I wish to lead: **Train, Empower, Acknowledge, Mentor**, and **Serve**. By serving others, we create a strong and cohesive team, much like a strong family characterized by communication, encouragement, enablement, and trust. Servant leadership found me like a spotlight in the desert night and shook me to my core. My purpose became simple, yet profound; **to serve others and help people achieve their full potential. To earn Invisible Medals.**

Much like defining our values so our values can define us, having a leadership philosophy is vital to our foundation.

Define your leadership philosophy, then allow your leadership philosophy to define and guide you as you lead.

10. What is your leadership philosophy?

Notes

1. *Rudolph the Red-Nosed Reindeer.* Rankin/Bass Productions. 1964.
2. McKinsey Quarterly. "Great Attrition or Great Attraction? The Choice is Yours." September 8, 2021. https://www.mckinsey.com/capabilities/people-and-organizational-performance/our-insights/great-attrition-or-great-attraction-the-choice-is-yours.
3. Chris Richie. "Try the TEAM Principle." Naval Institute Proceedings. 2001.
4. Zachary Martin, "Getting Serious about NCO Leadership," Marine Corps Gazette, January 2000.
5. United States Marine Corps, Command and Control, Marine Corps Doctrinal Publication 6 (Washington, D.C.: U.S. Government, 1989).
6. Jim Collins. *Good to Great: Why Some Companies Make the Leap and Others Don't.* (New York: Harper Business, 2001).
7. Wes Roberts, *Leadership Secrets of Attila the Hun.* (New York: Warner Books, 1987).
8. Teddy Roosevelt. https://www.goodnewsnetwork.org/. April 28, 2019.
9. Joe Byerly. "The Janitor who Helped put a Man on the Moon." From the Green Notebook. https://fromthegreennotebook.com/.November 24, 2017.
10. James Kouzes, *The Leadership Challenge* (San Francisco: Jossey-Bass Publishers, 1997).
11. Katherine Karvelas, *Winning with Teamwork* (New Jersey: Career Press, 1998).
12. Ibid.

Part Two

Captain Chris Richie addressing his Company, 2001

Leading with a Higher Purpose

Leadership

Photo of author, 2016

Chapter Five

Leadership

Leadership is action.
-John Maxwell

Leadership is deeply personal. Anyone who aspires to become a servant leader is driven by an innate desire to serve the needs of others. Before you can lead others, you must know yourself. That is where everyone's leadership journey begins. The first question on anyone's leadership journey is "Do you perceive yourself as a leader?" Every time I pose this question to a group, fewer than 20% of the audience-members' hands are raised. I then ask the group "Who thinks they will ever encounter another human being in their lives?" to which all hands are raised, along with a chuckle. I firmly believe that every individual reading this book possesses the potential to be an exceptional leader, regardless of their role as a parent, coach, boss, employee, or colleague. Leadership, as John C. Maxwell defines it, surpasses mere position, and emphasizes action.

Our daily interactions with people are ripe with opportunity to lead. As we continue our introspective journey to explore the essence of leadership and the profound transformative influence it can have through personal self-reflection, how do you define leadership?

11. What is your definition of leadership?

Every time I ask this question to students at Auburn University, the Air War College, or to people attending one of my workshops, I receive dozens of different answers. Although we may differ in our interpretation of leadership, every perspective is valid. In essence, there is no such thing as a wrong answer, and I have heard hundreds of definitions. Again, leadership is personal.

Your definition of leadership is not only how you wish to be led, but also how you wish to lead.

This diversity in understanding is what makes leadership so intriguing. My current definition of leadership is simply a **"relationship based on trust and consistent character."** Through introspection and self-reflection, I invite you to consider the type of leader you are or wish to be.

Let's begin by examining the characteristics of a **good leader**. A good leader positively impacts others through their actions, embodying the qualities of influence and service. Their focus is on generating positive outcomes. Take a moment to reflect on some leaders who positively influenced you. One of my first Marine Corps commanders was Brian Dingess. He was an incredible role model who embodied core values of family, faith, mentorship, and empowerment. Other leaders who greatly inspired me were Michael Rocco, Jon Davis, Robert Hedelund, Gary Thomas, Pete DeVine, Vincent Giani, Laura

Muhlenberg, Jeff Smith, Jimmy Clevenger, John Conrad, Gene Kamena, and Bill Lewis. The list could go on.

12. **Who comes to mind when you think of a good leader you have known? What leadership traits did they embody?**

_____
_____
_____
_____
_____
_____
_____
_____
_____
_____
_____
_____
_____
_____
_____
_____
_____
_____
_____
_____
_____

On the other hand, few people aspire to be a **bad leader**. However, there may have been instances when we negatively influence others. It is crucial to recognize such moments and strive to avoid them. For example, anyone familiar with Stone Mountain, Georgia will find the following story quite amusing. Stone Mountain can become extremely crowded when a large event is taking place, forcing travelers to park far away. On one occasion, my family arrived late during a July 4th celebration thereby requiring us to park in a satellite parking lot extremely far away. The conventional road leading us to the park seemed to be taking us the long way around, so I decided to lead my family on a shortcut through the woods, as the shortest distance between two points is a straight line, or so they say. We proceeded on this alternative path, walking and walking for a while until we encountered a large fence that blocked our path. It was impossible to climb over or go around. When I turned around, I saw approximately 20 people who had been following my lead, incorrectly assuming I knew precisely what I was doing. Reflecting on this rather embarrassing, yet amusing incident, I can assure you that my intentions were noble; however, I exhibited bad leadership. Unbeknownst to me, I was leading a group of people astray, thus negatively influencing the actions of those who had placed their trust in my navigational abilities.

This story serves as a reminder that people can unintentionally allow a negative attitude or their personal frustration to impact our interactions with others. The lesson is we should be ever mindful of our actions, realizing that others will follow our lead—negative or positive.

Be mindful of your actions, because people are always watching.

In contrast to bad leaders, **inspirational leaders** are individuals who motivate the actions of others. Gunnery Sergeant Dan Daly rallied his Marines during a fierce battle during World War I at Belleau Wood, France. Following the fifth failed assault, the Marines were ordered to conduct yet another assault. Sensing the dismay of his fellow Marines, Gunnery Daly stood up and belted out, "Come on you sons of b-----s, do you want to live forever!" [1] And with that, the Marines were inspired to charge the woods, and this time, they prevailed. We can never underestimate the power of inspiration. Inspirational leaders compel others to follow and inspire change. They may be found in various domains, such as servicemen and women, business leaders, authors, or even captivating movies that ignite our spirits.

Next, there is the **positional leader**. This is someone who holds a title or position of authority. Whether you are a parent or a teacher, positional leadership comes with inherent power. However, being a positional leader does not guarantee effective leadership. It is essential to wield authority responsibly and ethically. Two former Presidents captured this sentiment perfectly. President Abraham Lincoln understood that "Anyone can handle adversity; however, to test their true character, give them power." [2] During President George H.W. Bush's inauguration, he stated "There is but one true just use of power, and that is to serve others." [3] Anyone in a position of authority has been given an incredible opportunity to use that position for the benefit of others. Leaders must recognize this universal truth and acknowledge the gift of leadership, which is to serve.

Lastly, there is the **servant leader**. This type of leader builds relationships founded on trust and consistency of character. Trust is so important for leaders and has been described as the currency for building meaningful relationships. It can take years to build and a second to destroy. Consistency of character and positive influence are the measures of success for the servant leader. In my view, servant leadership is focused on caring for the needs of others. Nelson Mandela and Mother Teresa serve as notable examples, epitomizing compassion, humility, and forgiveness. As discussed in Chapter one, I view servant leadership in terms of earning invisible medals; helping people achieve their full potential.

13.   What type of leader are you?

_____

Good leaders exemplify habits aligned with personal values, and consistent ethical conduct. Teams place their trust in leaders who genuinely care for their well-being. The most successful organizations boast a strong and positive culture, fostered by leaders who inspire a shared vision and empower their teammates to achieve that vision. Leading with purpose and authenticity encapsulates all these aspects, and each one of us possesses the potential to embody all of them.

Are you leading in accordance with your purpose? The true essence in answering that question lies in whether your core values align with a greater sense of intention in your actions. We often hear about leading with intention and leading with purpose, but what does that really mean? Intentional leading requires deep reflection on who you are as an individual, as well as the moral values upheld by your organization. It involves identifying your personal values, the boundaries you will not cross. As this understanding grows, you engage in thoughtful reflection and act upon it. This is what it means to lead with intention and purpose.

Now, let's briefly explore our roadmap for Part Two and Three of *The Invisible Medal*, touching on crucibles and their significance, leading oneself with a focus on morals and values, leading others with an emphasis on ethics, leading teams where character plays a crucial role, and finally, leading organizations where culture takes center stage. In short, intentional leading will uncover your personal culture (Values, beliefs, artifacts, assumptions, character). You cannot unleash your full leadership potential until you unlock the door to your own consciousness. Be authentic; be you!

Lead with a higher purpose and earn Invisible Medals.

Leader Development Continuum

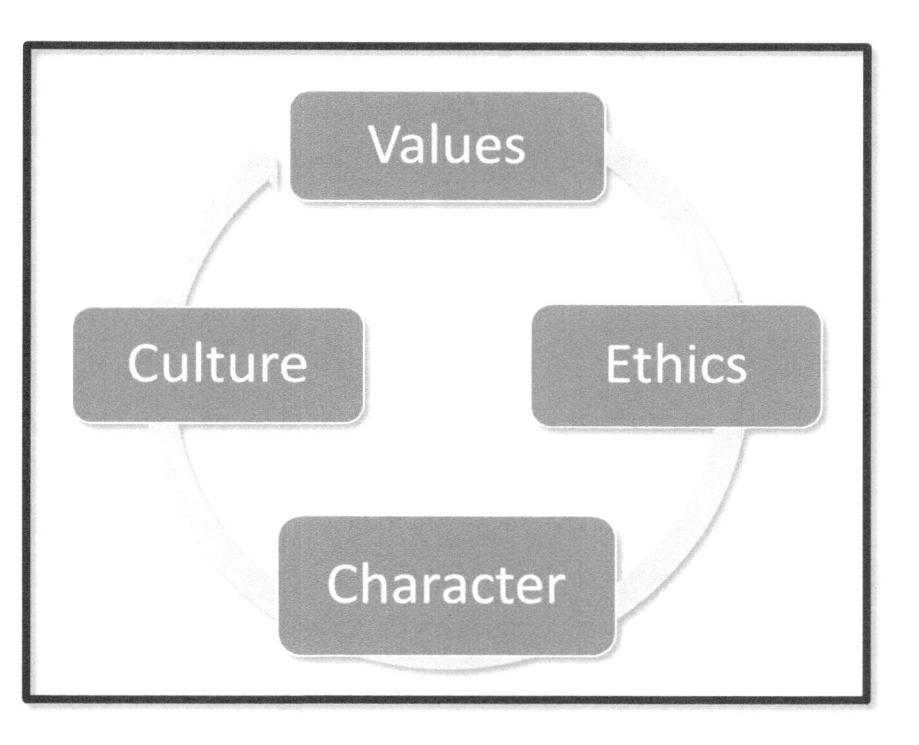

```
        Values
Culture         Ethics
       Character
```

          Leaders who seek invisible medals know how to lead with a higher purpose. They understand that unlocking their full leadership potential begins with finding their purpose and articulating their story. Reflection on one's purpose and story will reveal the foundational values that drive their actions and ethical behavior. Living in accordance with personal values and consistent ethical decisions reveals a leader's character which is a beacon that inspires others to follow. When people respect your character, they will listen to what you have to say because you have earned their trust. Conditions will be ripe for you to make an impact, to earn invisible medals.

Leading with a higher purpose can be achieved through what I call the **Leader Development Continuum**. The model is a continuum because there is no end to a leader's journey. Leaders continuously grow through life's crucibles and opportunities to strengthen their character and ethical behavior. The development continuum begins with **values** because values are formed in our youth and continue to be formed throughout our lives. Our unconscious actions are driven by strong feelings of what we believe to be right or wrong. Unlike values, **ethics** is a rational decision one makes outside of our feelings. Ethics weighs the pros and cons of any decision, recognizing that values have a part to play in decision-making. A person who consistently acts ethically and makes decisions in accordance with their personal values reveals their **character**. People follow leaders of strong character because they trust the leader's decisions will be made based on strong values and ethical reasoning. Leading with a higher purpose requires leaders to develop their own personal leadership **philosophy** which acts as the leader's accountability compass. Leaders with a philosophy that can be articulated to their teams demonstrate self-confidence in who they are and how they wish to lead. People like this are leaders worth following. **Culture** takes years to cultivate. Although most research on culture focuses on organizational culture, people who lead with a higher purpose understand that cultivating a personal culture is vital. A personal leadership culture cannot take root without an understanding of our values, ethical behavior, character, and a leadership philosophy. And it all starts with values.

Living in accordance with your values is the secret to leading yourself.

Notes

1. Charley Roberts. "Meet the Legendary Marine behind one of the most badass battle cries ever." Task and Purpose. www.taskandpurpose.com. March 5, 2022.
2. Abraham Lincoln. Quoted by SecDef William Cohen at United States Naval Academy commencement in 1999.
3. President George H.W. Bush said in his inaugural address on January 20, 1989: "Use power to help people. For we are given power not to advance our own purposes, nor to make a great show in the world, nor a name. There is but one just use of power, and it is to serve people"
https://avalon.law.yale.edu/20th_century/bush.asp

Values

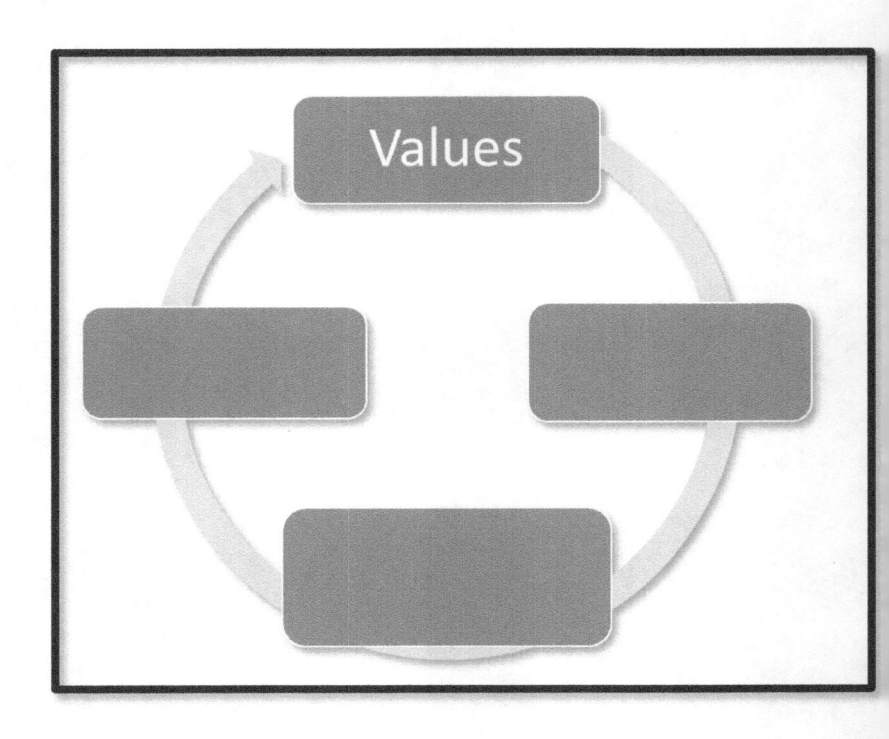

Chapter Six

Values

"The first and best victory is to conquer self."
- Plato

This statement by the ancient Greek philosopher Plato emphasizes the significance of self-leadership. Asserting that the most important triumph one can achieve is to master oneself, Plato implies that true leadership begins with inner discipline, self-control, and the ability to govern one's thoughts, emotions, and actions. His message serves as a timeless reminder that personal growth and self-leadership are vital in our journey towards success, fulfillment, and leading with a higher purpose.

The .25c Candy Bar and my first core value

At the tender age of 8, I experienced my first crucible and nearly lost an internal battle between right and wrong. My family resided in North Carolina, where I have fond memories of my grade-school years. One aspect I adored was the freedom to hop on my bike, traverse the main street from my neighborhood, and reach a nearby gas station. Armed with my occasional 25-cent allowance, I would indulge in the simple pleasures of purchasing candy-bars and baseball cards. In my young mind, it felt like a great adventure, as if I were embarking on a journey spanning a long distance. Little did I realize that the gas station was merely a stone's throw away, just across the street—a realization I now reflect upon with a chuckle. Funny how our young minds perceive size and distance.

On one fateful day, as I made my customary trip to the gas station, a sudden desire for a candy bar consumed me. However, upon reaching into my pocket, a sinking feeling settled in my gut—I had no money. The internal struggle began: the longing for that candy bar juxtaposed with the moral dilemma of not stealing. In a moment of weakness, I succumbed to temptation and slipped the candy bar into my pocket, exiting the store swiftly. As I pedaled my bike back home, I sought refuge in the solitude of my room to dispose of any evidence of wrongdoing. Yet, upon attempting to unwrap the ill-gotten treat, a sense of guilt overwhelmed me. This was wrong; I could not proceed with such dishonesty. Without hesitation, I returned to the gas station, retracing my steps to its exact location on the shelf, and restored the candy bar to its rightful place. As I departed, the cashier glanced at me knowingly, as if he had been aware of my internal struggle all along.

I consider this incident as the "25-cent candy bar that changed my life." Despite my initial transgression, my eventual corrective actions instilled within me a profound lesson on honesty and integrity which has become a core personal value I endeavor to uphold to this day. Although I knowingly violated moral boundaries, there was a core value—a firm line—that I refused to cross. Perhaps this value was instilled in me through Sunday school, my parents' guidance, or an innate sense of right and wrong. **The knowledge of right and wrong did not become a value until I experienced the choice between my knowledge and my actions.** That day taught me the significance of integrity, shaping my character, and influencing my actions ever since. Mahatma Ghandi so wisely summarized the importance of the epiphany that came to me in my youth,

First, we define our values, then our values define us. [1]

Morals and Values

Morals are beliefs which lie at the core of any society. In our intricate social order, we have established a framework of laws, standards of behavior, and principles that delineate what is permissible and what is not. However, these rules hold no significance until they align with our personal values. The convergence of our values with societal or organizational morals becomes the driving force behind our conduct, often serving as immutable boundaries that we dare not cross. People who wish to learn how to effectively lead themselves should reflect on the values that define who they are—a set of principles they would steadfastly uphold under any circumstances. To underscore the intersection of morals and values consider this question:

14. Why is murder universally regarded as wrong?

_____
_____
_____
_____
_____
_____
_____
_____
_____

Most people instinctively respond with "I don't know, it just is." However, from different perspectives, varying justifications emerge based upon one's personal values. Those with religious beliefs may point to the Ten Commandments, "Thow Shalt Not Kill," while proponents of natural rights theory may state that murder infringes upon the fundamental right to life. Despite divergent viewpoints and contrasting values, both arrive at the same moral conclusion. To further elaborate, the United States upholds the values of life, liberty, and the pursuit of happiness; however, individual perspectives and personal values may occasionally create conflicts, prioritizing life or liberty based on one's unique background and personal values. The interplay between perspectives and shared moral truths enables us to reconcile seemingly disparate viewpoints to find common ground. Two people with different values can uphold the same moral, thus making our understanding of values so important.

Values are the unwavering principles that define who we are and guide our actions. They form the bedrock of our character and violating them is inconceivable. If, by chance, we falter and act against our values, an overwhelming sense of remorse compels us to rectify our actions. You have most likely experienced such moments of introspection and growth.

True alignment occurs when our actions harmonize with our values.

When we are attuned to our values, they become the driving force behind our decisions and behavior. It is a synchronicity that evolves as we mature. In my earlier years, my focus was solely on excelling as a Marine, driven by the pursuit of success. Marriage bestowed upon me the aspiration to be a devoted husband, and parenthood further expanded my desire to be a loving father. Now, I find purpose in helping others achieve their full potential. Impact and significance have taken precedence over personal success, and my values have adapted accordingly. Change is natural and should be welcomed as we grow, and our values can mature along with us.

Several values hold special meaning to me, most of which came from observations or certain unexplained emotional reactions to various events. For example, humility emerged as a deeply held value while I was reading a book authored by a former appointed official. As I read the book, a negative reaction continued to come over me due to his excessive use of the words "I" and "me" taking credit rather than recognizing the value of people and teams. I never got through Chapter two and discarded the book. It became evident my focus lies in serving others, enabling their success rather than basking in personal glory. My value is focused on the success we can enable in other people. Thus, humility was identified as one of my core values—a guiding principle—which I consider to be a core value for any servant leader.

Values shape our character, define our leadership philosophy, and illuminate our path. Values serve as a roadmap to guide our actions, ensuring we remain true to ourselves. I learned the value of integrity/honesty at a very young age and the value of humility after I had already been a seasoned leader. In my current season of life, the following additional values serve as my compass: Faith, Family, Commitment, Loyalty, Trust, Teamwork, Relationships, Growth, Accountability, Respect, Professionalism.

15. What are your personal values?

If you had to prioritize them, could you? To help understand what you truly value, think of a time that you were filled with extreme happiness, or a time that you did something that was unpopular, because you felt it was right. Those memories combined with deep self-reflection will reveal your values.

During my leadership workshops and classes at Auburn University, I ask participants to reflect and write down their values and allow anyone to share who feels compelled to do so. Some popular values people often mention include Honesty; Service; Generosity; Empathy; Forgiveness; Trustworthiness. Whichever value you wrote down, I suspect there is a story behind that value. Again, YOUR values serve as YOUR compass. They will point you in the right direction and keep you accountable to yourself and those you are privileged to lead. Values will help you lead with a higher purpose.

The next time you find yourself getting angry over another person's actions, pause, and ask yourself, "Which one of my personal values did that person just cross?" I promise the level of understanding that will come from that moment of clarity will lead to much healthier discourse with others and resolve conflict. The more you live by your personal values, the stronger you will become as a person of character. Others will recognize you as a person whose actions are consistently played out in accordance with your values. If we do not think about our values and write them down, then how can we possibly act in accordance with them? For us to be defined by our values, we must first define them. As many renowned figures throughout history have quipped, "If we fail to plan, then we are planning to fail." [2]

Team Values

Another illuminating example of the power of values comes from the early days working for Auburn University and my Human Resource Development team. During an offsite session, we reflected on our purpose and the essence of our team. It was not an overnight revelation; rather, it took us two days of collective introspection. We discovered that our purpose resided in our unwavering belief in Auburn. It became the cornerstone of our mission and vision. Furthermore, as we explored our values, an intriguing realization emerged—our values spelled out the word "great." We determined our values to be **Growth**, **Relationships**, **Excellence**, **Accountability**, and **Trust**. This exercise underscored the power of values as our guiding compass for our team. We strive to live by these values and hold ourselves accountable to them so, in time, these words will become consistent values that will define the character of our team. The following month, during a very busy time for our team, one of our stakeholders requested some assistance. Despite our busyness, we chose to respond affirmatively, prompted by our core value of relationships. It became evident that our values serve as a compass, directing our actions and choices. I encourage you to embark on a similar journey with your team. It may be time to revisit and update your purpose, mission, vision, and values. Consider organizing a team-building event, such as an extended lunch, to engage in meaningful conversations about these crucial aspects of your team. You will witness the transformative power of such introspection and how it propels your team towards shared success.

16. What are your team's values?

_____

_____

_____

_____

_____

_____

_____

_____

_____

_____

_____

_____

Lessons from PFC Desmond Doss

Throughout history, one can find extraordinary stories of people who inspire us through their strong conviction in upholding their personal values. The remarkable story of Desmond Doss, immortalized in the film *Hacksaw Ridge*, serves as a powerful testament to the indomitable human spirit. Hailing from Lynchburg, Virginia, Doss embraced religious principles that forbade him from causing harm to another human being, regardless of the circumstances.

At the core of Desmond Doss's character was his commitment to serve his country. However, also at his core was the value of human life which presented a dilemma to the military recruiters when he chose to join the Army during World War II. Despite facing ridicule and skepticism, Doss's love for his country drove him to enlist in the military. He remained steadfast in his refusal to carry a weapon, resulting in his assignment to the medical corps. Amidst the taunts and jibes from his fellow Soldiers, Doss stayed true to his convictions, displaying the courage to live by the personal values that defined him.

It was on the battlefield of Okinawa, amidst the horrors of war, that Desmond Doss's true mettle would shine. As his large unit fell victim to a devastating Japanese ambush, chaos erupted. Amidst the turmoil, Doss made a resolute decision to remain on the hilltop, embracing his duty to save lives. In a display of extraordinary bravery, he selflessly rescued over 60 Soldiers treating both Japanese and American wounded without prejudice. His actions that day would forever change the course of countless lives.

Desmond Doss's unparalleled acts of heroism did not go unnoticed. President Truman bestowed upon him the prestigious Congressional Medal of Honor, a recognition reserved for those who display exceptional valor above and beyond the call of duty. Remarkably, Doss achieved this honor without ever wielding a weapon, distinguishing himself as a beacon of courage and compassion in the face of adversity.

Doss's steadfast commitment to his beliefs and values serves as an enduring lesson in leading yourself by upholding your personal values. A captivating scene in the movie occurs when the actor, Harvey Garfield portraying Doss says, "I can't live with myself if I don't stay true to what I believe." [3]. This statement encapsulates the profound impact personal values have in driving people to do extraordinary things. Doss's unwavering dedication to his principles highlights the depth of his character and the strength of his convictions to uphold his values. Desmond Doss inspires us all to stay true to our values and what we believe.

PFC Desmond Doss Medal of Honor Citation:

Private First Class Desmond T. Doss, United States Army, Medical Detachment, 307th Infantry, 77th

Infantry Division. He was awarded the Medal of Honor for conspicuous gallantry and intrepidity at the risk of his life, above and beyond the call of duty, in action against the enemy on Okinawa, Ryukyu Islands, 29 April - 21 May 1945. He was a company aid man when the 1st Battalion assaulted a jagged escarpment 400 feet high. As our troops gained the summit, a heavy concentration of artillery, mortar and machinegun fire crashed into them, inflicting approximately 75 casualties and driving the others back. Private First Class Doss refused to seek cover and remained in the fire-swept area with the many stricken, carrying them one by one to the edge of the escarpment and there lowering them on a rope-supported litter down the face of a cliff to friendly hands. On 2 May, he exposed himself to heavy rifle and mortar fire in rescuing a wounded man 200 yards forward of the lines on the same escarpment; and 2 days later he treated 4 men who had been cut down while assaulting a strongly defended cave, advancing through a shower of grenades to within 8 yards of enemy forces in a cave's mouth, where he dressed his comrades' wounds before making 4 separate trips under fire to evacuate them to safety. On 5 May, he unhesitatingly braved enemy shelling and small arms fire to assist an artillery officer. He applied bandages, moved his patient to a spot that offered protection from small arms fire and, while artillery and mortar shells fell close by, painstakingly administered plasma. Later that day, when an American was severely wounded by fire from a cave, Private First Class Doss crawled to him where he had fallen 25 feet from the enemy position, rendered aid, and carried him 100 yards to safety while continually exposed to enemy fire. On 21 May, in a night attack on high ground near Shuri, he remained in exposed territory while the rest of his company took cover, fearlessly risking the chance that he would be mistaken for an infiltrating Japanese and giving aid to the injured until he was himself seriously wounded in the legs by the explosion of a grenade. Rather than call another aid man from cover, he cared for his own injuries and waited 5 hours before litter bearers reached him and started carrying him to cover. The trio was caught in an enemy tank attack and Private First Class Doss, seeing a more critically wounded man nearby, crawled off the litter; and directed the bearers to give their first attention to the other man. Awaiting the litter bearers' return, he was again struck, this time suffering a compound fracture of 1 arm. With magnificent fortitude, he bound a rifle stock to his shattered arm as a splint and then crawled 300 yards over rough terrain to the aid station. Through his outstanding bravery and unflinching determination in the face of desperately dangerous conditions, Private First Class Doss saved the lives of many soldiers. His name became a symbol throughout the 77th Infantry Division for outstanding gallantry far above and beyond the call of duty. [4]

This citation not only represents the incredible bravery and selflessness displayed by PFC Desmond Doss during his service in Okinawa, but also the power behind people who know who they are, what they value, and the hardships we are willing to endure simply to be true to themselves. Doss epitomized Gandhi's statement of fist defining our values, then our values defining us.

His story is also a lesson in leadership. Desmond Doss was one of the lowest ranking Soldiers in the Army, yet, through his actions and commitment to personal values, he displayed the hallmarks of extraordinary leadership worthy of our admiration.

Failing Forward

Clearly the above story is a great example of success; however, what about stories of failure? As we pursue personal and professional growth, it is not only imperative to define the values that shape our character, but also essential to acknowledge that failure is an inevitable part of the human experience. We stumble, we falter, and we make mistakes because we are human. Yet, it is through these failures that we learn valuable lessons. When we fail, we must **fail forward**, by getting up, learning from our experience, and pressing forward. "Failure is the first step to success." [5] An exemplar of learning from failure is the legendary Michael Jordan, a name synonymous with basketball greatness. While we often perceive him as flawless, it is intriguing to discover that during his high school days, he was not selected for the varsity squad when an opening became available, losing out to a player who was much taller.

In the crucible of challenges, some may choose to abandon their pursuits, seeking solace in alternative paths of mediocrity or giving up altogether. Yet, the story of Michael Jordan offers a powerful lesson in attitude. Faced with perceived failure, Michael Jordan's mother urged him to persevere, to strive for improvement and uncover his true potential. That initial failure drove him to pursue excellence, not only eventually earning him a spot on the varsity squad, but also a spot in college and eventually in the professional league, where today, he is thought of as the greatest basketball player of all time. Jordan's remarkable quote resonates deeply with what it means to fail forward:

I've missed more than 9,000 shots. I've lost almost 300 games. 26 times, I've been entrusted with the game winning shot and missed. I have failed over and over again in my life. and that's why I succeed. [6]

Failures are a prime example of a leadership crucible. If approached with the right mindset, these challenging experiences become invaluable opportunities for growth. They will test our mettle and reveal our capacity to learn. When faced with setbacks, do we succumb to defeat or choose to rise above? Consider Thomas Edison, the Wright Brothers, Steve Jobs, and countless others who learned from their "failures," to create the modern world.

The first time I applied for my current job, I was not selected, but I remained grateful for the experience and the opportunity to even be considered. I maintained a positive attitude, sent a thank you note to every member of the search committee and interview teams and remained hopeful some other opportunity would materialize. Three months later, I received a phone call informing me that the other candidate had not made it past the probationary period and the job was mine if I still wanted it. This serves as a poignant reminder:

Life is filled with unexpected twists and turns. Our ability to embrace failure and press forward is instrumental in our journey towards success.

Moreover, it is crucial to recognize that wisdom and inspiration can come from anyone, regardless of age or rank, just like PFC Desmond Doss. I have gleaned profound insights on leadership from the younger Marines I have had the privilege to serve with. It is a testament to the fact that learning knows no boundaries or preconceived notions of job title or position. Allow me to share a touching anecdote involving my daughter, who, through her tireless dedication, earned a place at Auburn University as a member of the flag-line and prestigious Tiger Eyes. Despite her accomplishment, she returned home after her first grueling 10-hour practice, visibly disappointed. Perplexed, I inquired, only to discover her resolute commitment to improve. When I told her to come inside, eat dinner, and get some rest, she replied, "No, dad, I'm not good enough. I couldn't do what the other girls were doing, and I need to work harder." My daughter sought to match the abilities of her peers, and tirelessly continued to practice in our driveway, under the cover of darkness. This profound display of perseverance and unwavering attitude when faced with perceived failure, left an indelible mark on my understanding of leadership. The following morning, I thanked my daughter for

"...teaching this Marine Colonel a thing or two about perseverance and attitude." Yes, I am a very proud Dad who has been Blessed with two strong-willed daughters who regularly teach me lessons in leadership.

> **Our attitude is our personal internal dialogue which exerts a tremendous influence on our journey towards greatness or mediocrity.**

17. Identify times when you failed. What did you learn about yourself?

_____
_____
_____
_____
_____
_____
_____
_____
_____
_____
_____
_____
_____
_____
_____

Amidst the competing voices of optimism and doubt, it is paramount to choose a positive narrative that propels us forward, even after we have failed. Attitude becomes the differentiating factor, separating the ordinary from the extraordinary. When embraced as a catalyst for growth, failure becomes a steppingstone towards success. I encourage you to cultivate a mindset that sees failures not as defeats, but as crucibles that teach invaluable lessons. Harness the power of a positive attitude, and you will achieve excellence.

Most values are born from personal experience and upbringing, life's crucibles, and even our own emotions. Reflecting on the above allows us to understand our feelings and why we react the way we do under various circumstances. Identifying our values and understanding why they exist is the first step toward self-actualization and learning to lead ourselves.

The stories of PFC Desmond Doss, Michael Jordan and even my daughter serve as powerful reminders of resilience and determination that define exceptional leaders who have conquered themselves by defining their values, upholding their values, and learning to fail forward. It is imperative that we take the time to define our values, or we will not be able to allow our values to define us, which is the first step to leading with a higher purpose. What Plato summarized so long ago remains true today, "the first victory is to conquer self," and there is no better way to conquer self than to know what you believe and the values that define you. Once we fully understand our values and embody them in our actions, we are ready to learn to lead others with consistent ethical behavior and decision making.

Notes:

1. Mahatma Ghandi. Quote discovered through Bing AI on December 19th, 2023.
2. Several variations of the statement "Failure to plan is planning to fail" have been attributed to dozens of people. It is unknown who first made this universally true statement.
3. *Hacksaw Ridge*. Lionsgate Summit Entertainment. 2016.
4. Medal of Honor Citation. PFC Desmond Doss. www.cmohs.org.
5. Fo Alexander. "6 Reasons why Failure is the First Step to Success". www.Clevergirlfincnace.com. May 7, 2023.
6. Michael Jordan. www.goodreads.com.

Ethics

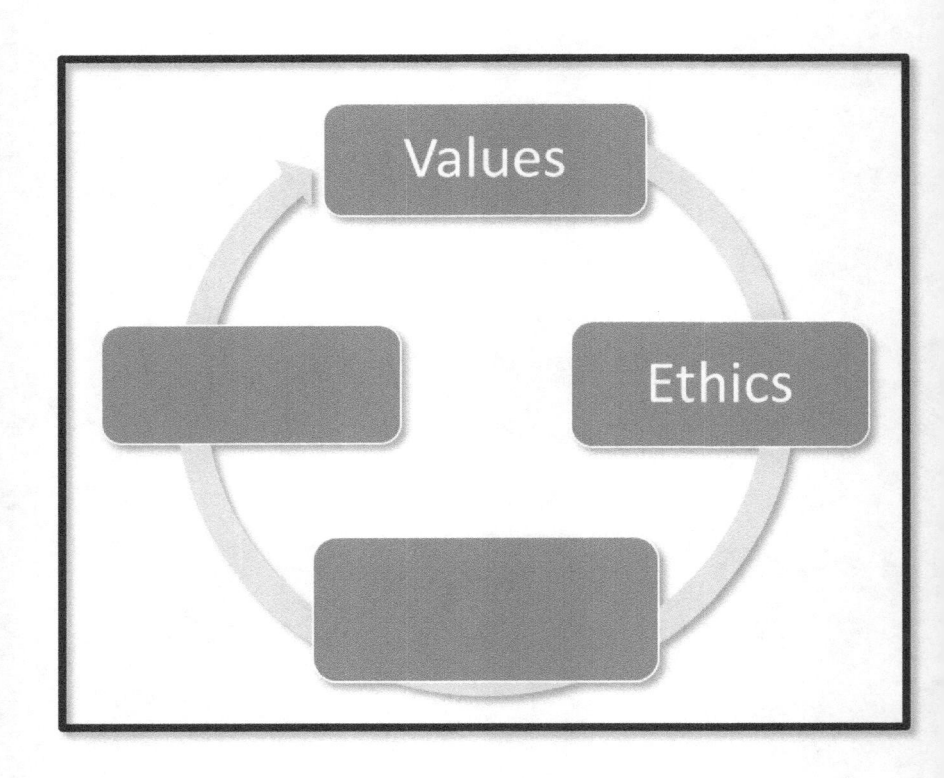

Chapter Seven

Ethics

"A leader is one who knows the way, goes the way, and shows the way." - John C. Maxwell

Congratulations! You have taken the biggest step in leadership which is to know yourself. You have reflected on past events and crucibles that helped you better understand who you are and what you value. You have built the foundation of how you will lead others. Let's assume you are a new supervisor where for the first time, you are responsible for one or more human beings.

Your very next step is to stop thinking about your success. Care for those under your charge and build trust in those you are now privileged to lead.

A proven method to earn trust is to be consistent with your actions in keeping with your core values and to display consistent ethical behavior and decision-making.

Aristotle endeavored to live in accordance with the virtues of prudence, justice, temperance, and courage. He believed that possessing these virtues made a person good, happy, and flourish. He espoused these behaviors as virtue ethics. Virtue is defined as behavior showing high moral standards. The most important word in this definition is "behavior." Behavior is your values and ethical decision-making manifested into actions on full display. People who demonstrate consistent values with thoughtful ethical decision-making truly inspire others to follow. Consider the world-renown golfer, Bobby Jones.

Bobby Jones is a name that will forever be associated with the game of golf. His achievements in the sport are legendary as is the name of the golf course he created, Augusta National. When Bobby Jones was praised for calling penalty strokes on himself, his response demonstrated his high morals, values, and ethics: "You may just as well as praise me for not breaking into banks. There is only one way to play this game." [1] The movie, *Bobby Jones, Stroke of Genius* beautifully portrays one such occurrence. His virtuous behavior was truly inspiring and serves as an example of how to uphold our values by consistent ethical behavior.

Leaders can positively influence others once they have earned trust in those they lead. Leading oneself requires a clear understanding of societal and organizational morals as well as individual values that serve as redlines not to be crossed. Leading others requires disciplined adherence to those values and sound ethics when tough decisions must be made. And doing so consistently.

Effectively leading others requires a person to exhibit uncompromising ethical behavior so a trusting relationship can be built. We should never underestimate the importance of ethical behavior and how it impacts those we lead because leaders are always on full display.

If our actions and decisions do not align with our espoused values, few would have the desire to follow us.

How many times have we observed a boss telling us to do something only to find them not adhering to the very rules they set? I bet dozens. It is very difficult to trust someone like that.

I remember the moment that drove this point home for me. Shortly after 9/11, I was leading a team on deployment in the Middle East. Upon arriving, we met with personnel from a small Air Force unit who had been deployed for several days preparing the base that we would call home for the next eight months. All of them were unshaven. During our first staff meeting, one of our Marines asked if we were allowed to forego shaving, given that we were in the field with just 135 people out in the middle of nowhere. In other words, no one would know. My response to this question was simple yet firm: "Are you a United States Marine? Yes, sir. Then shave your face." I reminded him that we live by certain standards, and there was no reason to deviate from those standards of discipline just because we were in a remote location and could "get away with it."

Over twenty years after this incident, I found myself teaching a seminar at the Air War College, when an Air Force Lieutenant Colonel approached me to reveal that he was a young second lieutenant in that same Air Force unit and was present at that staff meeting when the Marine asked about shaving. He revealed that he was embarrassed to be unshaven and said that my response had a significant impact on his leadership philosophy for the next 20-plus years, which was based on discipline and accountability, and acting in accordance with his values.

This interaction reminded me that our actions, even seemingly small ones, can have a profound impact on others. People are always watching what we say and do and can be positively (or negatively) influenced by our behavior. It is crucial for leaders to set a positive example by upholding high standards and doing what is right, even when it is difficult because you have no idea the impact you will have on others by your actions.

Even little things like having a smile on your face can go a long way to comforting a person who may otherwise be experiencing stress or anxiety. I observed this regularly with my children when they were very young. Being from Alabama, my wife loved dressing our girls in smocked dresses with hairbows and taking them with her everywhere. The times I would accompany them to the grocery store, we would inevitably walk by someone whose facial appearance made it clear they were having a bad day. Then as we approached and they took one look at our girls, their facial reaction would change from a frown to a beaming smile. They could not help it. People have the same opportunity to turn someone's frown upside down simply by taking the time to smile or acknowledge them. In fact, this anecdote alone demonstrates how anyone has the capacity to influence others. We have significant opportunity during our interactions with others—people we know or have never seen before—to positively influence them in some way.

Leaders are responsible to set standards for our teams and to live up to those standards ourselves. We must be willing to do the hard things and make difficult decisions not based on popularity but based on values and ethical logic. It is important to remember that our actions and decisions have a lasting impact on those we lead, and we must always strive to lead by example. To that end, we must be mindful of our morals, values, and actions. Our actions matter. By setting a positive example and upholding high standards, we can inspire and influence others to do the same. The epitome of setting a good example is manifested through our ethical decision-making.

Ethical Decision-Making

Ethics is a fascinating subject because it is neither a value nor a moral. Ethics is not a matter of right or wrong and feelings will not help when it comes to making an ethical decision. Some argue that ethics exists independently of our emotions, that it is a reality that requires thoughtful decision-making based on morals and our values to guide our actions. Much like crucible events, ethical dilemmas are a part of everyday life, and are colored in shades of gray. Often, the decisions we make may not be popular and will upset or alienate others, especially when our only available option is choosing between two wrongs. At best, your decision will upset someone. At worst, your decision may violate one of your values, fracture trust, or turn people against you. Dr. Jack Kem introduced the Ethical Triangle as a framework to help us overcome ethical dilemmas. [2] His ethical triangle consists of three components: principle ethics, consequence ethics, and virtue ethics.

- **Principle ethics** involves decisions that are fundamental, pure, and unquestionable.
- **Consequence ethics** aims to produce the greatest good for the greatest number of people.
- **Virtue ethics** centers on the Golden Rule, treating others how we want to be treated.

Dr. Kem's triangle is such a helpful tool for leaders that experience ethical dilemmas.

Ethics over Values

Leaders will face difficult ethical dilemmas that may cause conflict with a personal core value. To illustrate, the following story describes an ethical dilemma I faced as a seasoned Company Commander. In the Marines, integrity is the top core value, one that cannot be violated. Lying at the Naval Academy, OCS, or Boot Camp is grounds for immediate dismissal. Integrity matters. During a deployment to an undisclosed location, our organization faced a tense situation while setting up in an unfamiliar location with the responsibility of providing our own internal security. Amidst our preparations, there was an individual from the host nation who persistently irritated us, exhibiting rude and inconsiderate behavior towards our Marines, some of whom were female.

One of our younger Marines (a Lance Corporal) approached me, expressing frustration with the situation and asked if something could be done. I decided to handle it diplomatically by addressing the issue with the individual's superior. In my weekly meetings with the foreign officer who oversaw the base, I shared our concern and requested that action be taken to alleviate the annoyance. The following day, to our relief, the individual was no longer present. With the distraction removed, we could focus on our mission.

However, a week later, the base Commander shared an unexpected turn of events. The individual we had reported was undergoing severe mistreatment, having been subjected to confinement and deprivation of human necessities. The officer expressed his desire to speak with the person who reported the incident to me because he wanted to verify the authenticity of the claims before taking "even more severe disciplinary actions that would impact him and his family." Realizing the potential consequences for the individual involved, I went back to our site and approached the Lance Corporal, explaining the situation.

I discussed the cultural context with him, emphasizing that extreme measures were taken to save face when actions causing embarrassment occurred in that culture. While I would not order him to lie, I laid out the potential outcomes if he chose to do so. **Clearly, we both had come face to face with**

an extreme ethical dilemma. Together, we drove back to the base commander's office, where under questioning, the Lance Corporal admitted to fabricating the story, citing a bad day and a lack of enthusiasm for being away from home. Surprisingly, I found myself convinced by his performance and even questioned the authenticity of his original claim.

When the Lance Corporal finished his tall tale, the base commander was visibly angry, telling the young Marine to leave as I steadied myself to get an "ear full." I accepted the scolding, acknowledging the consequences of my actions. After leaving the office, I informed the Lance Corporal that he should hereby consider himself "sufficiently punished" and that neither of us would likely forget this experience. I expressed my remorse for the turn of events and the ethical crucible involving integrity; however, I believed that we had significantly reduced someone's suffering; thereby, placing the value of human life above the value of integrity. The Lance Corporal agreed. Our mission remained intact, and everything proceeded smoothly for the remainder of our deployment. The instigator of our troubles returned to his duties the next day and no further taunts were ever directed our way.

This incident taught me a valuable lesson: ethics can overpower even the strongest of values or can reveal an even stronger core value. In that crucible moment, it was the value of prioritizing a fellow human being's life and well-being that superseded our commitment to integrity. The Lance Corporal and I upheld Dr. Kem's virtue ethics from his "Ethical Triangle." Though it was a difficult decision, I never lost a minute of sleep over it. If faced with a similar situation, I would make the same choice without hesitation because ultimately, the preservation of life is paramount.

18. Have you ever experienced an ethical dilemma? What did you learn about yourself (your values, virtue, ethics)?

Ethical Crucibles

Leaders are often faced with difficult decisions that require us to weigh our values against the potential consequences of our actions. It may be tempting to take the easy way out or to ignore ethical considerations, but ultimately, the decisions we make reflect who we are and the values we hold dear. Our observed behaviors will determine whether we have earned the trust and right to lead others.

When making decisions, it is important to consider not only the ethical triangle (consequence, virtue, and principle), but also what we can live with based on alternate realities of what might happen resulting from our decision. This process is like playing chess. You must look at moves and counter moves, second, third and fourth order effects, and then go back and start over again and again until you finally arrive at a decision that results in checkmate.

Values can often feel emotional while ethics is more stoic; however, making ethical decisions can be challenging, especially when the potential consequences are severe. You must consider the potential risks and rewards of different courses of action and make the decision that aligns with your values or upholds an ethical principle, realizing those two may not always align.

It may be tempting to make decisions most popular with your team or to ignore difficult ethical dilemmas. Do not fall for it. In the long run, it is always better to be honest and truthful with a clear understanding of our personal values and ramifications of the ethical decisions we make. Leaders must always strive to do what is right, especially when it is difficult.

I recently recalled an ethical crucible involving my daughter and her friend. As they were leaving an apparel shop, her friend discreetly took a hat and concealed it under his shirt, leaving my daughter feeling panicked and unsure of what to do. She urged him to return the stolen item, but he adamantly refused. In that moment, she made a difficult choice. Instead of continuing with their plans to go out to eat, she decided to take him home, as she was "not feeling well." However, her integrity and strong sense of right and wrong compelled her to drive back to the store alone. She courageously approached the store staff and explained what had occurred, taking responsibility by paying for the stolen hat. I was deeply impressed by her actions. The hat cost $40, but I gave her $80 as a token of appreciation for her ethical decision. At the age of 18, she experienced a crucible never to be forgotten and the value of integrity emerged as a core personal value. I expressed my pride in her and commended her for upholding her value of integrity, ethics (virtue, principle), and the law even though it may have damaged a relationship with a friend (value). It is remarkable how children can sometimes teach us such valuable lessons.

This incident also made me reflect on the person she has become and the importance of staying true to our values and making ethical choices. Let it serve as a reminder that our decisions shape our character and reflect who we truly are. Take the time to reflect and learn from your ethical crucibles, as they can contribute to your growth as a leader and as an individual. Remember, the decisions you make reflect who you are and the values that define you. So, take the time to reflect on your ethical crucibles and what you have learned from them. By doing so, you can become a better leader and earn invisible medals.

The Ethical Dilemma of Dropping the Atomic Bomb

During World War II, the decision to drop the atomic bomb on Japan was a major ethical dilemma for President Truman and his advisors. The strategy of unconditional surrender was difficult for military personnel because it required unleashing everything on the enemy until they capitulated. A commonly held belief was that the Japanese would fight to the last man, woman, and child, which posed a challenge for Truman's advisors who had been planning for an island invasion.

President Truman formed a committee of advisors to decide whether to proceed with dropping the bomb. The advisors faced a collision of morals, values, and ethics when considering the consequences of such an action. On one hand, dropping the bomb would end the war quickly, but it would also result in massive destruction and civilian casualties. On the other hand, invading Japan would result in significantly more casualties on both sides resulting from a prolonged invasion.

19. If you were a member of the advisory group, what would you have recommended and why?

If you were President Truman, would you have made the same decision?

Leaders must consider values, consequences, virtues, and ethics when making difficult decisions. Truman's decision to drop the atomic bomb was one of the most difficult decisions made by any leader in history. It is easy to make recommendations, but the ultimate decision and its consequences must be weighed heavily by the leader with ultimate decision authority. President Truman drove this point home with his famous desktop plaque simply stating, "The buck stops here." Although morals and values played a key role in the discussions, in the end, it was **consequence ethics** that won the argument, and the rest is history.

The lesson here is that leaders must be prepared to make tough decisions that can have a significant impact on the lives of others. It is essential to consider all possible outcomes and the ethical implications of each decision. Leaders must weigh the potential consequences and make the decision that aligns with their values and ethics, even if it is not the easiest choice. And they must do so with consistency. In terms of questioning decisions that have been made, one must be willing to put themselves in the shoes of the decision-maker. In doing so, one can better understand the weight of their decisions and the potential consequences of their actions. It is through this understanding that leaders can make decisions that align with their values and ethics, and that will benefit their organizations and society.

During my research, I asked ChatGPT to provide an example of an ethical dilemma. The AI response is quite interesting, and I believe accurately describes what we humans undergo when difficult decisions must be made:

> As an AI language model, I have not experienced ethical dilemmas in the same way that humans do. However, I have been programmed with ethical guidelines to ensure that I produce ethical and responsible responses. I prioritize respecting human dignity and diversity, avoiding harm, promoting well-being, and being transparent about the limitations of my abilities. In general, ethical dilemmas arise when one has to choose between two or more conflicting values or principles. It can be challenging to make a decision when different values are at stake. However, it is essential to reflect on one's values, ethics, and decision-making processes when facing ethical dilemmas. It is also crucial to consider the potential consequences of each option and evaluate what one can live with. In conclusion, while I have not experienced ethical dilemmas, I have learned that it is essential to prioritize ethical guidelines in my responses to ensure that I promote responsible and ethical behavior. [3]

Unlike artificial intelligence, humans are consistently presented with decisions which frame the bedrock of what is called **character**. Our character is revealed by the consistency of our actions in harmony with our espoused values. Consistency of character matters regardless of our position or industry we find ourselves in.

Notes:

1. Bobby Jones. Our Favorite Bobby Jones Quotes. https://www.bobbyjoneslinks.com/.
2. Jack Kem. Ethical Decision Making: Using the "Ethical Triangle". U.S. Army Command and General Staff College. https://cgscfoundation.org/wp-content/uploads/2016/04/Kem-UseoftheEthicalTriangle.pdf.
3. ChtGPT question posed on October 23, 2023.
4. John Maxwell. *The Five Levels of Leadership*.
5. Winston S. Churchill. https://www.goodreads.com/quotes/550356-you-make-a-living-by-what-you-get-you-make. This quote has also been attributed to Arthur Ashe.
6. Gbenga Adebambo. Hire Character. Train Skills. The Good Men Project. 2018. https://goodmenproject.com/business-ethics-2/hire-character-train-skills-cmtt/
7. President Theodore Roosevelt. https://www.goodnewsnetwork.org/theodore-roosevelt-quote-about-reputation/
8. Warren Bennis. www.bing.com. The quote "Leaders define reality and inspire hope" is attributed to Warren Bennis, a renowned scholar in the field of leadership and organizational studies. His work emphasized the importance of visionary leadership and the role leaders play in shaping the future. Bennis believed that effective leaders not only understand the present reality but also inspire others by painting a compelling vision of what could be.
9. Henri Nouwen. https://quotefancy.com/quote/1926753/Henri-J-M-Nouwen-I-have-always-been-complaining-that-my-work-was-constantly-interrupted
10. The phrase "Visibility creates stability" was introduced by Chief of Space Operations Gen. B. Chance Saltzman. He proposed the concept of "Competitive Endurance" to ensure U.S. access to space and prevent competition with space powers like China and Russia from escalating into conflict or crisis. www.bing.com.
11. John Maxwell. *Becoming a Person of Influence: How to Positively Impact the Lives of Others*. Harper Collins. New York, New York. 2006.

Character

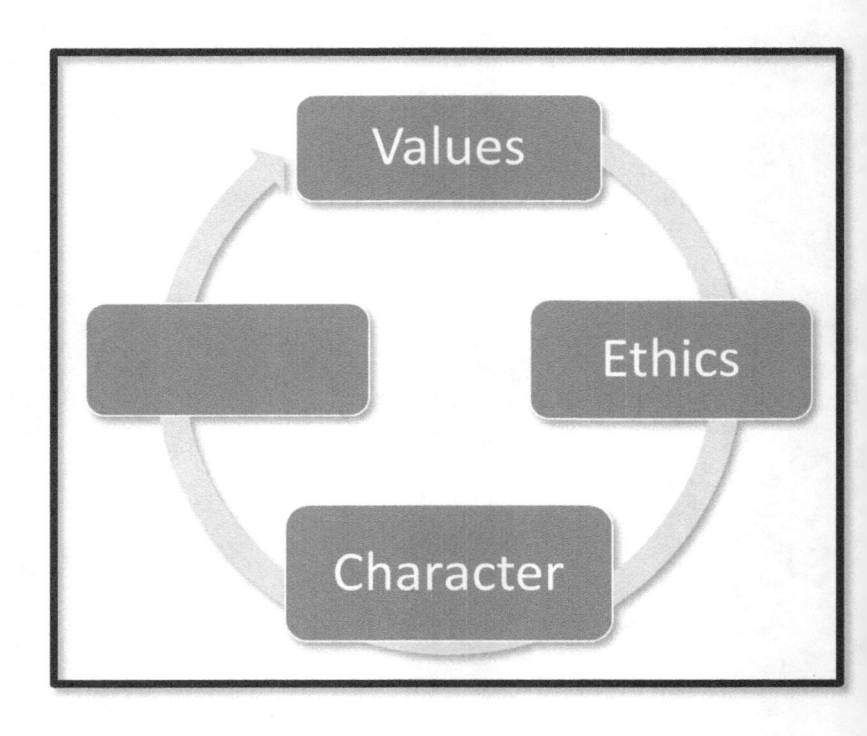

- Values
- Ethics
- Character

Chapter Eight

Character

"Character is destiny." - Heraclitus

I have been intrigued by the subject of character for most of my adult life. **Character is a leadership multiplier.** Character is the foundation for any human being. Being a person of character is the cornerstone of how I choose to serve any team I am privileged to lead. I draw inspiration from the root word of character which is "char," loosely translated to "engrave." Can you envision a master sculptor chiseling the words on a tombstone that epitomizes and immortalizes the person he wishes to define. Just as Heraclitus stated, character is indeed our destiny. Character cannot be faked. Any leadership position must be embarked upon free of bias or ulterior motives. Understanding your identity and purpose is paramount to growth and your leadership journey. Who are you as a leader? What is your purpose in leading others? How would others define your character? It is crucial to understand these introspective questions to establish a solid foundation for who you are and how you wish to lead.

Character is an essential element for anyone charged with leading a team. A person of strong character will inspire people to achieve greatness. Taking charge of a team provides incredible positional power which can be used for good (enable and empower a team) or bad (beating down your team). President Lincoln's enduring quote on character, power, and challenges serve as a reminder that "Nearly all men can stand adversity, but if you want to test a man's character, give him power." [1] When you are privileged to lead a team, let your character shine by treating everyone with dignity and respect, let your teammates know they matter and bring value to the team, and how everyone contributes to the team's success. Therein lies true power.

A prime example of leading with character can be found in the popular Apple television series *Ted Lasso*. The humble character, Ted, grapples with numerous dilemmas and demonstrates valuable leadership lessons through his journey of overcoming adversity. He had the positional power of leading

AFC Richmond as the coach, yet his focus was on building personal authority by investing in his players, club owners, assistant coaches, and even an adversarial press. Everyone associated with his team mattered. Everyone was valued. Ted was a person of character who put the needs of his players, coaches, and his family above his own needs. Ted helped people believe in themselves and believe in each other captured by a moving scene when he tapes the word "Believe" above his office door. [2] Consider watching this show for insightful lessons in leading with character. After years of serving in leadership roles, *Ted Lasso* provided me a welcome reminder to ensure every member of my team knows they are valued and serve a vital purpose for our team's success.

So, how does one become a person of character? Thankfully, in 1993, President Reagan perfectly answers this question during his commencement speech at the Citadel.

> Character takes command in moments of crucial choices. It has already been determined. It has been determined by a thousand other choices made earlier in seemingly unimportant moments. It had been determined by all the little choices of years past. By all those times when the voice of conscience was at war with the voice of temptation whispering the lie that it really doesn't matter. It has been determined by all the day-to-day decisions made when life seemed easy, and

crises seemed far away. The decisions that piece by piece, and bit by bit, developed habits of discipline or of laziness, habits of self-sacrifice or of self-indulgence. Habits of duty and honor, and integrity or dishonor and shame. Because when life does get tough, and the crisis is undeniably at hand. When we must in an instant look inward for strength of character to see us through, we will find anything inside ourselves that we have not already put there. [3]

Reflecting on President Reagan's profound words, one cannot help but be moved by his call to action to be tuned in to all our small actions which help us become a person of upright character.

Inherent motivation lies in recognizing that our character is the culmination of our habitual choices.

The ancient philosopher Aristotle encapsulated this truth succinctly: **"We are what we repeatedly do."** Every action, every decision, holds significance because they contribute to the building blocks of who we are. Consider the impact of these choices on the perception of others. Are we consistently punctual or habitually late? Do we prioritize the well-being of those around us or are we self-focused? Are we known for our trustworthiness and integrity or for our deceitfulness and dishonesty?

Character serves as the bedrock upon which our leadership philosophy is built.

The significance of character cannot be overstated in the realm of leadership. By intertwining character with vision, we equip ourselves to lead effectively and inspire those around us to achieve that vision. Let us remember that our character is forged not only in the critical moments in front of others, but also in the silent battles when we are alone. It is through cultivating positive habits and embodying traits of honor, integrity, ethical decisions, and selflessness—especially when those crucibles hit us—that we strengthen our character.

Leaders of Character Must C-A-R-E

During my first month in my first (and hopefully last) post-military retirement job, it was clear I was experiencing a difficult transition. Although I was comfortable in my role as leader in a small, yet extremely impactful and highly functional team, feelings of self-doubt due to unfamiliar territory occupied my thoughts. Starting a brand-new profession after serving as a Marine for three decades was daunting. Several questions permeated my mind such as, "How can I do well in a job for which I have little experience?" Of course, military service prepares us to be good leaders; however, military leadership and civilian leadership are not the same, or so I thought. Rather than focusing my thoughts on self-doubt, I reminded myself of the fundamental aspects of leadership in any profession. In short, **being a person of character** who focuses on people and building meaningful relationships. To live in accordance with my values and consistent ethical behavior.

I was also reminded of John Maxwell's research into his five levels of leadership model and the sad fact that 80% of today's supervisors are stuck at level 1, characterized by a person who will use their position to coerce and punish others through fear. [4] Simply put, a level 1 leader does not lead, they boss because they are self-focused. I think those who remain at this level lack self-confidence, and simply do not trust or care for others. We have all likely experienced a boss who acts in this manner. Any new boss automatically starts at level 1 until their actions start to speak volumes on how they view themselves and others.

A person of character will not remain in level 1 very long. People of character will take seriously the words of Winston Churchill who stated, "You make a living off of what you get, but you make a lifetime from what you give." [5] In summary, a leader's role exists to serve the needs of others; to earn Invisible Medals. In time, people of character will learn the skills required for their job and, along the way, will have built strong relationships with their team.

> **Your title makes you the boss;**
> **Your character makes you the leader!**

On my first day in my new profession, I endeavored to live by one of my favorite statements by the former President Teddy Roosevelt first introduced in chapter four, "People will not care how much you know, until they know how much you care." This quote has always inspired me to focus on people as I try to be the best leader in whatever role I found myself. In terms of application, however, there is no roadmap to articulate precisely how to show your team that you genuinely care. I discovered that a sincere effort to **Communicate**, be **Available**, be **Respectful**, and **Encourage** others (C-A-R-E) was a good path to follow. In short, new leaders who wish to connect with their team, to demonstrate character, and to build relationships must CARE.

Communicate

Renowned military leader, Napoleon articulated that the fundamental role of a true leader is "To define reality and give hope." [6] I am an optimist by nature and always view the glass as half-full; however, this can sometimes be off-putting to a team who understands the reality of bad situations because they have been there before. Let's face it, sometimes the reality of a bad situation is just that, Bad! This is where a good leader steps in to communicate one of the most powerful words in human lexicon, **Hope**. To be honest, my first month came with challenges and some of our "realities" had multiple barriers. Slowly, our team began to overcome the barriers until a path became clear. We arrived at that path because we collectively saw a better future and built bridges instead of accepting roadblocks. Hope motivated us to move forward together.

Be Available

The author and priest, Henri Nouwen was moved by a fellow priest who admitted that in his younger years he would despise the interruptions by his team as he tried to work; "I have always been complaining that my work was constantly interrupted; then I realized that the interruptions were my work." [7] Learning a new job is time consuming and requires countless hours of reading policy, turnover binders, e-mails, etc. All of this requires time alone to process, take notes, and prepare, but we must not forget that **visibility creates stability**. During this period, your team desperately wants and needs to get to know you. Expectations must be articulated, and relationships must be built. As much as I wanted to learn everything about my new job, my focus had to be on the people who would be the ones to help me thrive (or fail) in my new role. Just as Henri Nouwen observed, our first and foremost job should be **people and relationships**. For the majority of my first month, this was time well spent.

Be Respectful

Every human being is unique. We all come from varied diverse backgrounds to include differences in our political viewpoints and religious beliefs. Far too many people are quick to argue their personal viewpoint and look down upon those who do not think the same way. I prefer to look upon my teammates through the lens that Martin Luther King Jr. taught us by judging others solely by the content of their character. For some, this will be difficult until they understand their own bias and reflect upon why they think the way they do. As much as we believe certain things; others feel just as strongly in their beliefs. Rather than attempting to push our own beliefs on others, perhaps we should be respectful of diverse viewpoints, and enjoy personal growth in the process.

Encourage

In his book, *Becoming a Person of Influence*, John Maxwell tells us that to become a person of influence, "...you have to come alongside them and really get involved in their lives." [8] The Marine Corps states it more succinctly, "Know your Marines." This goes far beyond simple job performance and means a leader must understand the goals and passions of others in both their personal and professional lives. Only then can a leader encourage someone to achieve their full potential. Encouraging others can be so refreshing, especially when we see that smile on their face and spark in their eye. When this happens, you know they are inspired to put their best foot forward. One of my favorite verses is Proverbs 11:25, "He who refreshes others will himself be refreshed." I have found this to be so true the times I have positively encouraged other people along with the joy of earning invisible medals. Once you observe a teammate take that first confident leap forward, you feel as though you are leaping with them; what a great feeling!

No one person owns the undisputed best definition of leadership. And rightly so since leadership is personal. Everyone has a separate and unique leadership path. During my 53-year leadership journey, I have grown, reflected, matured, and sometimes faltered. My current season in life has taught me that **leadership is simply a relationship built on trust**. A leader's trust can be earned in several ways; I try to follow the path of communicating, being available, being respectful, and encouraging others. Showing my new team that I genuinely C-A-R-E will take time and consistency. It is a long path that I look forward to traveling.

20. Think of a time when you were a member of a high performing team. What were the characteristics of that of the team leader?

_____
_____
_____
_____
_____

During one of my deployments, I observed remarkable character by a Sergeant in charge of a small team of eight Marines in Nicaragua. His actions taught me the enduring character traits of **initiative**, **teamwork**, and **humility**. The following story was first published by the Marine Corps Association in the July 2020 edition of the Marine Corps Gazette. [9]

Lessons on Character from Nicaragua

Every Marine volunteered to serve our nation when they chose to become a United States Marine. As promotions occur, Marines earn the right to lead a larger number of fellow Marines. Over time, a spirit of selfless service and leadership virtues become synonymous with a Marine's character. Through training, observation and repetition, leadership traits and principles simply become a part of who we are. I have had the privilege to lead Marines, but more importantly, I have had the honor to serve with countless leaders of all ranks who have inspired me to be a better officer. One such display of unforgettable leadership took place in 2010 in the most unlikely of places, Nicaragua.

The circumstances that brought me to Bluefields, Nicaragua in September 2010 were completely different than the circumstances which brought Marines here on several previous occasions throughout the contentious history of our two nations. [10] We did not come to protect U.S. interests or to support a rebel force seeking to overthrow their government as had occurred when Marines last landed in Bluefields. Our Special Purpose Marine Air Ground Task Force (SPMAGTF) was on a 10-day mission to conduct military exchanges and provide security for various Non-Government Organizations (NGO) and medical teams conducting humanitarian activities throughout the country. [11] With our history, it is no surprise that our welcome by the Nicaraguan Navy was lukewarm at best.

As I walked through the impoverished community of El Bluff near Bluefields on the first day of our military-to-military engagement, I could not help but reflect on "Chesty" Puller and Smedley Butler whose actions here are legendary. Their mission was to secure and defend; our mission was to protect and build (partnerships). Later that evening in the wardroom (dining facility) aboard the USS *Iwo Jima* (LHD 7), I noticed one of our NGO teammates who seemed upset, so I asked to join her. I learned she was disappointed because the U.S. Embassy had not coordinated a school for her to deliver the hundreds of backpacks and supplies as part of her "Give a kid a Backpack" organization. I immediately thought of El Bluff and put her in contact with one of our Marines, providing commander's guidance for him to investigate options. Six days later, I listened as she enthusiastically briefed the Command deck on what our Marines had done. As she told her story, I was filled with pride to learn of the character displayed by our Marines. Through their quick **initiative**, unselfish **teamwork** and genuine **humility**, our Marines changed hearts and minds as they planted the seeds for strong partnerships to grow.

Initiative

In *The Servant*, James Hunter asserts "Each of us has the capacity to make a difference in another person's life, and this is especially true for those of us in leadership positions." [12] The small group of eight Marines in the ranks of Lance Corporal to Sergeant epitomized Hunter's statement. For the first couple days of their military exchange, the Nicaraguan Navy personnel treated our Marines with apathy; the school principal treated them with distrust; the community treated them as unwelcomed guests. One might expect the Marines to lack the motivation to assist; however, their reaction was the exact opposite. In less than 8 hours, they coordinated with the school principal and Nicaraguan military to buy into their plan. The solution included a small Nicaraguan boat to come alongside the *Iwo Jima* to receive hundreds of supplies and transport them to the school. For many, a backpack filled with school supplies sounds insignificant; however, for such a poor community, this gesture yielded unsurpassed gratitude. The Marines did not simply take the initiative to accomplish a task. **They took the initiative to make a difference.**

The Marines understood that when you make a difference in the life of one person, they will carry that home to their family, to their friends, perhaps even to their co-workers. Your influence will lead them to influence others and before you know it, there will be an entire wake of positive energy created just because you cared. Their initiative was motivated by a strong desire to make a difference, which makes this unique leadership story more compelling.

Teamwork

The small team of Marines jumped at the opportunity to not only work with the NGO and civilian populace of El Bluff, but also sought ways to include their Nicaraguan counterparts. The principal postponed school for a few hours to conduct a ceremony, with the rest of the community observing as the backpacks were delivered to each child. The general scheme of maneuver called for the Marines to remove the backpack and hand it to the NGO representatives who would hand the backpack to the child. On their own accord, the Marines decided to give that honor to their Nicaraguan military counterparts. In fact, as the ceremony began, the Marines removed themselves from the limelight altogether. They felt this was a moment for the community to share.

Following the ceremony, the Nicaraguan's gratitude could not be understated as—with tears in their eyes—they told our Marines what it meant to have been given the opportunity to be viewed as heroes in the eyes of their community. We learned that despite their poverty, the community provided the Naval personnel with food, gifts, and acceptance. The military personnel at El Bluff did not have the means to do anything in return for the kindness they received. In other words, for the first time, they were the ones taking care of the community instead of the other way around. **They felt valued as contributing members of the community.**

It was clear by their demeanor that this simple act of enabling them to be a part of the team was worth more than any military exchange ever could be and set the stage for a true partnership to emerge. These Marines looked past the ambivalent treatment and pressed forward. Their sincerity led to acceptance which turned into teamwork. In a short period, their initiative led to the formation of an ad hoc team that worked together to accomplish a unified objective.

Humility

Our nation's history books speak of a stormy relationship between Nicaragua and the United States so it should have been no surprise that our engagement with the Nicaraguans initially fell flat. My commander's diary entry on 17 Sep states, "The military receptions have been lack-luster, as if they really don't want us here." [13] This all changed on 23

Sep following the ceremony at the school. When our Marines were seen as people who cared to make a difference and had the desire to enable others, another trait was demonstrated: humility. Humility is not a trait usually associated with the Marine Corps warrior ethos; however, humble leaders not only gain the respect of others; humble leaders inspire. World-renown leadership author and servant leader Ken Blanchard captures the essence of humility, "Humility may seem at odds with the image of the heroic, powerful leader. Instead of worrying about how powerful they are, servant leaders focus on what others need." [14]

A seasoned leader of character understands that humility is the first step to building a meaningful relationship.

The Marines' innate character allowed them to seize an opportunity to make a difference in people's lives and they capitalized on it. When the Marines humbly took a step back and included the Nicaraguan Naval personnel, our international partners felt appreciated and valued. A 10-day country engagement is not long enough to build a long-term relationship, but it is a start. There is a saying I heard during our deployment which states, "Those who give will someday forget, but those who receive will always remember." [15] When we return to Nicaragua, I trust the community of El Bluff will remember and greet us as partners. This budding partnership was made possible by a small group of Marines whose initiative, teamwork and humility set conditions for a future relationship to grow.

When we arrived, we were greeted with malevolent looks and an attitude of animosity. We departed with handshakes and an attitude of respect and appreciation. Eight young Marines turned potential mission failure into complete mission success simply **by the virtue of their character.** They not only salvaged our military exchange, but they also enabled success for an NGO to brighten the day for hundreds of children. Fourteen years after their actions, I still recall the valuable leadership lessons from Nicaragua and how Marines with initiative, teamwork and humility impacted lives and truly made a difference. They taught me how character can indeed be "destiny." My experiences in Nicaragua taught me to embrace the lessons of initiative, teamwork, humility, and the impact that your character can have on others.

Haiti: A Lesson on Character

During this same deployment, I encountered yet another prime example of character during a frightening turn of events in Haiti. Just like the previous story, the following story was also first published in the Marine Corps Gazette. [16]

Nothing seemed out of the ordinary on the morning of 30 July 2010 as I made my way to the landing force operations center; however, the look on our operations officer's face told me this was not a normal morning.

> Sir, we just heard from the GCE [ground combat element] commander; he said Medical Site 2 is being overrun by a mob of approximately 1,000 Haitians. We have not been able to reestablish communications with him.

Several thoughts ran through my mind upon hearing such news. Our 505-Marine Task Force was embarked aboard the USS *Iwo Jima* just off the coast of Port de Paix, Haiti, and only a few miles from Medical Site 2. Thirty-three Marines had been operating for six days from the nearby United Nations (U.N.) compound while providing security, convoy, and logistics support for two medical sites and two engineering sites. [17] The Marines' actions over the next several minutes were nothing short of awe-inspiring. Below is an excerpt from a note I sent to my chain of command the following day:

> Fourteen Marines arrived ... to find large numbers of Haitians gathered. Initial reporting indicated a hostile crowd of 1,000 people. The GCE Commander dispatched another Squad to reinforce. We fragged an aircraft to insert the only remaining interpreter (all

others were on site) and to conduct airborne ISR [intelligence, surveillance, and reconnaissance]. When the interpreter arrived, he observed over 20 Marines with arms interlocked holding back an angry crowd of 300 people. Prior to this, a UN security guard used OC spray [pepper spray] which incited more anger. Ten Haitian Police attempted to disperse the crowd with their batons; however, our Marines persuaded them to let us maintain control peacefully. The local police were asked to pull the primary agitators out of the crowd and off the premises. Shortly thereafter, the medical site began to see patients, which calmed the crowd. Afterwards, our interpreters spoke with the crowd. The general perception was that the Marines protected the Haitians from further OC spray and from being beaten by the Haitian Police. The Marines on site gained great respect and admiration from all. Of note, the police were amazed at the Marines' ability to control the crowd without using our weapons and asked to be trained in crowd control. I could not be prouder of the Marines' actions and courage under these conditions. Every Marine had their T/O [table of organization] weapon; at no point did anyone go from Condition 4. [18]

A vastly outnumbered group of Marines averted a potentially devastating event and turned what would have been a story broadcast worldwide into a story never told. They displayed hallmarks of Marine Corps leadership through detailed **preparation**, undaunted **courage**, and impeccable **character**.

Preparation

As reveled in Chapter One, I grew up greatly respecting my grandfather who served as a company commander in the Philippines and survived the Bataan Death March and over 3 years as a prisoner of war. He would often tell me to hope for the best but always prepare for the worst. Heeding his advice, exactly 65 days prior to the event in Haiti, Marines were completing a mission rehearsal exercise that culminated with a quick reaction force charged to subdue an angry crowd via non-lethal means. This training was led by a staff sergeant whose actions in Haiti helped save the day. Additionally, in the weeks leading up to our mission in Haiti, Marines were given rules of engagement (ROE) classes based on realistic vignettes. We were not preparing for combat; we were preparing to maintain order for ill parents, children, and grandparents who sought free medical care provided by the U.S. Navy and NGO partners. Detailed preparation led to multiple discussions on ROE and expectations of acquitting ourselves as strong, professional, and compassionate warriors. It helped greatly that we had six

Marines who had been raised in Haiti and spoke fluent French Creole. They became our pseudo cultural awareness instructors as we conducted final preparations. Following the event, the CP-10 commander sent a note to his boss including the comment that:

> The Marines treated the people respectfully and addressed the situation professionally, and the situation was defused. (Of note, the SPMAGTF trained to this scenario during their field exercise prior to deploying and their training kicked in and kept everything well within control.) [19]

Preparation for worst-case scenarios instills confidence and fosters courage.

Courage

Marines are no stranger to Haiti. In the early 1900s, experiences there helped drive doctrine rediscovered in the *Small Wars Manual*, which espouses tolerance, sympathy, and kindness. [20] To be effective as a peacekeeper, Marines have learned they must first be respected as warriors. After 100 years of operations in Haiti, the word Marine has become synonymous with courage where we are well respected throughout the country. At the age of 16, one of our translators, Staff Sergeant Merci, was so impressed by observing Marines (near Port au Prince) that he wanted to become one, which he did. His actions on 30 July 2010 were noteworthy.

When acts of compassion are displayed by those who are strong, they are truly inspiring. As the Haitian National Police drew batons to assault the crowd, a Marine gunnery sergeant exhibited strong leadership and courage by not only stopping them, but in perfect French Creole, he told them to leave; they complied without hesitation. The Marine was operating from a position of authority that had been earned by generations of Marines before him.

Following the incident, several people in the crowd approached our Marine translators thanking them for protecting them from the police; the police approached our Marines asking them to train them in how to respond via non-lethal means. Courage breeds compassion; compassion from those in power breeds authority. In *The World's Most Powerful Leadership Principle*, James Hunter discusses power versus authority:

> Power is the ability to force or coerce others to do your will because of your position or might; Authority is the skill of getting others willingly to do your will because of your personal influence. [21]

He further asserts that authority is about who you are; authority is about character.

Character

The Marine Corps' 31st Commandant often spoke of the "three block war" concept. In addition to being men and women of character, he adds, "... decisions will be moral quandaries whose resolution requires a high degree of maturity, discretion, and judgment." [22] The angry crowd grew even more incensed after a U.N. security guard pepper sprayed them. Just as circumstances had reached critical mass, and in the absence of riot control equipment (shields, baton, etc.), a staff sergeant (the same one who conducted the riot control training two months earlier) directed a human chain to be created. The Marine translators began walking the lines communicating with the people while one translator unpacked a bull horn and began directing the crowd. In a fine display of both courage and teamwork, Marines from the rank of lance corporal (an assault amphibious vehicle mechanic) to second lieutenant (aviation command and control) interlocked arms to form the human shield with weapons at sling arms.

The best method for leaders to "ingrain the qualities of character" in our employees is to embody the virtues of impeccable character ourselves.

All Marines displayed courage and strong character following the lead of their officers and SNCOs. After the incident, the Navy commander in charge of Medical Site 2 provided the following commentary:

> If the Marines were not here, we could not accomplish the mission at all. When we rolled in, there were 3,000-5,000 patients. If you take the Marines out of the equation, none of this happens. [23]

One of the public affairs officers concluded that "a rifle on the shoulder did not send the wrong message; it helped people get the right care." [24] In response to the event on 30 July, one general officer commented that this was "just another example of what we do around the world every day."

Marines all over the globe are conducting themselves with distinction, many in combat zones, yet their stories are rarely told. They are simply being themselves; they are upholding the ethos articulated by our 13th Commandant that "the term 'Marine' has come to signify all that is highest in military efficiency and soldierly repute." [25] Leaders must prepare their teams for worst-case scenarios, while exhibiting personal examples of courage and character. Although the actions of a few Marines at Medical Site 2 were noteworthy, it was hallmarks of Marine Corps leadership displayed by every Marine present that made the difference on 30 July 2010.

The Ripple Effect of Character

Just as a stone thrown into a lake creates ripples that seem to have no end, leaders, through acts of kindness and selflessness, can create positive ripples that extend beyond far beyond our immediate surroundings. True leadership is measured by the growth and success of those we lead, and it all boils down to leading with character. People of character encourage and uplift those around them. Through visible leadership and consistent character, leaders create an environment where individuals are empowered to act, thereby fostering a culture of trust and accountability.

The famous American artists, Norman Rockwell and Richard Sargent captured 1940s-1960s Americana on the covers of the magazine, *Saturday Evening Post*. On the March 20, 1954 cover, Richard so accurately captures the dark side of the ripple effect with an angry boss yelling at his employee. The employee goes home and yells at his wife, who then yells at her son, who then yells at the cat. [26]

Bad leaders create negative ripples. Leaders of character create positive ripples.

Anytime we have a bad day at the office, human nature dictates we will come home with those ill feelings. We subconsciously act out those feelings around those who mean the most to us.

In other words, the way people are treated at work is the way they will treat others, including their family. Leaders should remember this truth every time they interact with their employees, co-workers, and even their boss.

Let's create positive ripples!

My stories from Auburn University, Nicaragua and Haiti reveal how character plays a vital role in leading teams, even during crisis. By embracing the values of **initiative, teamwork, humility, preparedness,** and **courage,** leaders can demonstrate **character** and cultivate a winning organizational culture. Leaders who C-A-R-E (**Communicate,** are **Available,** are **Respectful,** and **Encourage**) will earn the trust of those they are privileged to lead. By implementing these principles, leaders can lay the foundation for resilient organizations that thrive even in the face of adversity.

Understanding your identity, purpose, and character lays the groundwork for effective leadership and sets you and your team on a journey towards greatness. It is through the fusion of character, values, and ethics that leaders and their teams achieve remarkable outcomes. By embarking on an introspective journey and aligning your actions with your purpose and values, you create a strong compass that guides your decisions and fosters a culture of excellence.

Lead with Character!

Notes

1. Abraham Lincoln. Quoted by SecDef William Cohen during the United States Naval Academy commencement address in 1999.
2. *Ted Lasso*. Apple TV. 2020-2023.
3. President Ronald Reagan. Commencement speech at The Citadel, 1993.
4. John Maxwell. *Five Levels of Leadership: Proven Steps to Maximize Your Potential*. FaithWords, Brentwood, TN. 2011.
5. Winston Churchill. The Socratic Method Blog. https://www.socratic-method.com/quote-meanings/winston-churchill-we-make-a-living-by-what-we-get-but-we-make-a-life-by-what-we-give. This same quote has also been attributed to Arthur Ashe.
6. Howard Graham. The Center. "Leaders Define Reality and Offer Hope." https://www.thecentermemphis.org/resources/leaders-define-reality-and-offer-hope. September 7, 2020. Quote attributed to Napoleon.
7. Henri Nouwen. https://henrinouwen.org/
8. John Maxwell. *Becoming a Person of Influence: How to Positively Impact the Lives of Others*. Harper Collins Leadership. New York: New York. 2006.
9. Chris Richie. "Leadership Lessons from Nicaragua". Marine Corps Gazette. July 2020.
10. In 1910, Smedley Butler led Marines at Bluefields to protect U.S. citizens and support Nicaraguan rebels. In 1926 Marines landed at Bluefields to protect U.S. citizens and fight a group led by Augusto Sandino later referred to as the "Sandinistas once again." In 1985, LtCol Oliver North was involved with the "Iran-contra affair" where the U.S allegedly sold arms to Iran to fund contras (Rebel insurgents) in the hopes they would take over the leadership of Nicaragua from the socialist Sandinistas. More details are specified in Max Boot's book, The Savage Wars of Peace. Small Wars and the Rise of American Power. Basic Books, New York, New York. 2002.
11. Operation CONTINUING PROMISE was a single-ship (USS Iwo Jima) humanitarian mission conducted from July-November 2010 in Central/South America.
12. James Hunter. *The World's Most Powerful Leadership Principle. How to become a Servant Leader*, Crowne Business, New York, 2004.
13. Taken from notes in my Commander's Diary. SPMAGTF-CONTINUING PROMISE Deployment, July-November 2010.
14. Ken Blanchard. *Servant Leadership in Action. How you can achieve great relationships and results*. Berrett-Koehler Publishers, Oakland, CA. 2018.
15. Quote attributed to a Colombian officer during our 10-day engagement with the Colombian Marines.
16. Chris Richie. "SPMAGTF Leaders in Action, Another Example of What we Do." Marine Corps Gazette. August 2012.
17. Taken from CP-10 Haiti Warning Order, dated 23 July 2010.
18. E-mail sent by author on 31 July 2010. Condition 4 means the weapon is safe with no magazine or round inserted in the chamber.

19. E-mail sent from Commander, CP-10, to Commander, Navy South, 30 July 2010.
20. U.S. Marine Corps, Small Wars Manual, Government Printing Office, Washington, DC, 1940, reprinted 1 April 1987 by Headquarters Marine Corps.
21. James Hunter. *The World's Most Powerful Leadership Principle: How to Become a Servant Leader*, Crown Business, New York, 2004, p. 53.
22. General Charles C. Krulak. "The Leadership Imperative," foreword in Corps Business by David Freedman, Harper Collins Publishers, New York, 2000.
23. From Defense Video & Imagery Distribution System at http://www.dvidshub.net/ video/ 93128/spmagtf-supports-continuing-promise-2010.
24. Ibid.
25. Headquarters Marine Corps, United States Marine Corps Manual, Article 38, Washington, DC, 1921 edition.
26. Richard Sargent. "Saturday Evening Post," March 20, 1954.

Part Three

Roots of Success

Culture

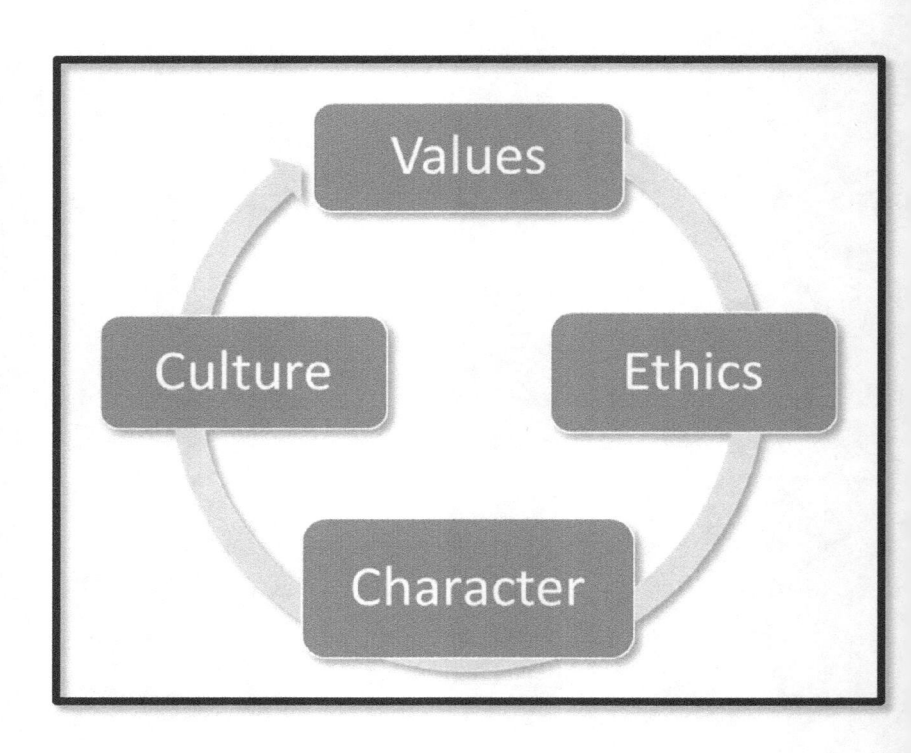

Chapter Nine

Culture

"Culture eats strategy for breakfast."

- Peter Drucker

The intent throughout this book has been to discover how to unleash our full leadership potential (**leading self with values, leading others with ethical behavior, leading teams with character**). Our leadership journey starts with an inward focus on personal values, our ethical decision-making, and our character. Combined, all these attributes drive the creation of our personal **leadership philosophy**. For most people, leading a team may be the pinnacle of our opportunity; however, many may find themselves leading at an even higher level. The pinnacle and final level of leadership beyond ourselves, others, and teams, is when we find ourselves at the helm of leading an organization. This level requires leaders to craft, strengthen, or create an organizational **culture** built for long-term success.

Cultural Roots

Derived from the Latin word meaning "to cultivate," culture reflects organizational values and observed behaviors that—when properly cultivated—allows organizations to thrive. However, if culture is neglected or taken for granted, organizations can whiter and fail.

Character defines an individual; culture defines an organization.

Whereas servant leadership is described as earning invisible medals, culture is described as the roots of an oak tree. Above ground, we see a majestic tree; however, it is the roots which we do not see that determines whether the tree will flourish or fail. Similarly, culture (roots) enables organizations (oak tree) to stand upright, strong, and resolute when the storms of life come. Strong roots allow the tree to grow and flourish, to become stronger. Weak roots will not allow the tree to withstand even the smallest storm. Cultural roots matter and will determine success or failure for any organization.

The renowned leader and author Peter Drucker, once stated that "culture eats strategy for breakfast." [1] This powerful statement emphasizes that no matter how well-crafted a strategy may be, it is the organizational culture that ultimately shapes their legacy. **Culture is the underlying force that guides employee behaviors, decision-making, and alignment with organizational mission and goals.** Senior leaders must recognize that an effective strategy is only as strong as the culture that supports it. In some cases, we observe the leader's character is so strong, that their personal beliefs are imbued within the organization's culture. Leaders who understand and cultivate a strong organizational culture will drive positive change and achieve long-term success. In this chapter, we will explore the significance of culture in organizational leadership, drawing inspiration from various examples and insights. From the wise words of Peter Drucker to the remarkable stories of companies and institutions like Southwest Airlines, Chick-fil-A, Auburn University, and the United States Marine Corps, we will explore the power culture has in shaping an organization's destiny.

Culture encompasses the collective beliefs, values, norms, and behaviors shared by members of an organization. Culture extends to the vision, mission, and purpose that drives decisions and actions. It shapes employee interactions, customer experiences, and overall organizational identity. For example, what images or thoughts come to mind when you hear the words Wal-Mart, Publix, Auburn University, Southwest Airlines, Chick Fil-A, or the United States the Marine Corps.

To gain a better understanding of culture's powerful influence, let's compare the cultures of two well-known companies: Walmart and Publix. When discussing Walmart, thoughts often revolve around low prices and vast product selection. However, Publix is associated with exceptional customer service, cleanliness, and a focus on relationships. Both companies have distinct cultures that align with their respective visions and missions. Understanding these differences highlights the impact culture has on customer perception, employee engagement, and overall organizational success.

A strong organizational culture is intricately linked to the organization's vision, mission, and purpose. For instance, Publix's purpose revolves around relationships, while Walmart aims to provide the lowest cost. These divergent visions drive the development of distinct cultures within each organization. Leaders must ensure that the culture they cultivate aligns harmoniously with the organization's vision, serving as a compass for decision-making and strategic direction.

21. **Identify the differences between Wal-Mart and Publix**

<u>WalMart</u>

<u>Publix</u>

Publix's mission is "To be the premier quality food retailer in the world." A visit to their website reveals their top commitment is a "focus on customer value" and even asserts they will "never knowingly disappoint." [2] I experienced Publix's culture firsthand in May 2022. When I stopped by the store to pick up flowers I had ordered as a gift to my family for my retirement ceremony, I was told the order had been misplaced. The store manager responsible for the florist greeted me very kindly and apologetically. Rather than dismissing my problem, he owned the problem with me. Since I had no time to wait due to the preparation for our ceremony, the manager offered to deliver the flowers to my home less than an hour later, which he did, no additional charge. A year later, I stopped by the store to ask the manager if he could share more information with me about this book. When I asked if I could include his name, he told me, "No," simply stating that his actions would have been the same for ANY manager at any Publix. "That is just our culture." Wow! Such actions cannot be taught, they must be lived and displayed daily. I for one am a loyal customer, despite their higher prices.

On the other hand, Walmart's mission is to "help people around the world save money and live better." [3] These divergent visions and missions lay the foundation for the distinct cultures within each organization. Whenever I want to make a quick trip to a store to buy something I know will be at a reasonable price, and do not have any desire to speak to anyone, I go to Wal-Mart. Nonetheless, despite living near both Walmart and a Publix, I frequently choose to drive the extra mile to Publix. Why? Because I know that I can rely on Publix to offer a clean environment and helpful assistance when I need it, albeit at a higher price. Whether it's locating a specific item, like Coleman's mustard (which is tucked away in a peculiar section alongside British delicacies) or receiving personalized guidance, Publix never fails to deliver. Unlike the automated self-checkout systems that dominate many stores, Publix emphasizes the human touch. They even go beyond having just one cashier per register; they have two—a person to assist you and another to handle bagging. And that's not all—they even offer to help carry your groceries to your car, no tips allowed. These small yet significant differences set the cultures of Walmart and Publix apart. However, it is important to note that neither culture is inherently superior to the other. It all comes back to the organization's vision and purpose, which serves as the guiding principles driving their respective cultures. Prices are indeed higher at Publix, but you are not just buying a product, you are paying for a quality experience. Wal-Mart's cost-cutting measures always deliver products desired by the consumer at the best possible price.

War Eagle and the Auburn Creed

The famous Auburn University rallying cry, "War Eagle," carries deep significance for the Auburn family. An incredible story stemming from a golden eagle retrieved from a Civil War battlefield, the power of this phrase resonates with the legends and traditions that unite us. On a recent overseas trip, I was surprised with eleven different greetings of "War Eagle" from complete strangers. Years earlier, I had similar encounters in the Dubai International airport, the Santa Monica pier, the deserts of the Middle East, and countless locations around the globe. These encounters remind me of the profound impact culture has on organizations. Auburn's spirit of camaraderie and shared identity serves as a testament to the importance of fostering a sense of belonging—even among strangers—through symbolic gestures, phrases, and common values (The AU Family).

Equally symbolic of Auburn's culture is the "Auburn Creed." An icon to Auburn University history, at the age of 77, George Petrie wrote the words that forever captured the beliefs and values of our great institution. Deteriorating health associated with age and the passing of his beloved wife Mary, led George to retire in 1942 from the university he faithfully served as professor, coach, Dean, and administrator for 53 years. His spirit was uplifted in 1943 by one of his former associates, A.B. Moore who wrote,

Men make institutions. The character and traditions of every institution are largely determined by a few stalwarts who give their all to it. Your years of distinguished service to Auburn...constitute one of its greatest assets. Your name will always be associated with its success and best traditions...The greatest possible comfort and pleasure to parents in their old age is the knowledge that their children are respectable and doing well. You have a host of intellectual children. [4]

A.B. Moore gifted George Petrie with an **Invisible Medal** that lifted his spirits thereby motivating him to reflect on his time at Auburn, and draft the words now immortalized as the Auburn Creed.

The Auburn Creed was first published in a front-page article in the Auburn Plainsman on January 21, 1944, and resonated deeply with anyone associated with Auburn University. An amazing anecdote is captured in the foreword of the book, *Auburn Man*, by Mike Jernigan. The son of the revered Auburn coach Ralph "Shug" Jordan shares a story of a conversation he had with his dad. Shug explained to his son that the Auburn Creed epitomized the spirit of our beloved institution. He writes,

He first learned of the "Auburn Creed" while in the Army during World War II. An unnamed friend sent him a copy in the spring of 1944, and he had that copy with him a month or so later when he landed in France on the beachhead at Normandy. [5]

The stories of "War Eagle" and the AU Creed highlight the vital role that culture plays in our organizations. By fostering a sense of unity, celebrating our shared stories, and staying true to our core values, we can create a culture that leaves a legacy.

The Auburn Creed

I believe that this is a practical world and that I can count only on what I earn. Therefore, I believe in work, hard work.

I believe in education, which gives me the knowledge to work wisely and trains my mind and my hands to work skillfully.

I believe in honesty and truthfulness, without which I cannot win the respect and confidence of my fellow men.

I believe in a sound mind, in a sound body and a spirit that is not afraid, and in clean sports that develop these qualities.

I believe in obedience to law because it protects the rights of all.

I believe in the human touch, which cultivates sympathy with my fellow men and mutual helpfulness and brings happiness for all.

I believe in my Country, because it is a land of freedom and because it is my own home, and that I can best serve that country by "doing justly, loving mercy, and walking humbly with my God."

And because Auburn men and women believe in these things, I believe in Auburn and love it.

-George Petrie (1943)

A Leader's Role in Culture

Senior leaders understand the power of culture and the importance of aligning culture with vision. The relationship between culture and leadership is akin to two sides of a coin—intertwined and inseparable. When leaders step into their role, they have the power to shape and influence the existing culture. In the book, *Good to Great*, Jim Collins states that the best leaders "…channel their ego needs away from themselves and into the larger goal of building a great company." [6]. Beware of those leaders whose hubris will drive them to attempt to change the organizational culture to match their personal beliefs and values. Strong organizations can fend off such actions; however, weak organizations will fall victim. Perhaps you have experienced the positive impact of a leader who takes a good culture and propels it forward. In such cases, progress becomes the order of the day, a continuous journey of improvement and innovation rather than regression and stagnation. Conversely, there are cultures so remarkable, like the United States Marine Corps, that altering any facet seems unnecessary. These exceptional cases demonstrate the essence of a culture so rich and thriving that it remains untouched, an embodiment of excellence. The intricate dance between culture and leadership underscores the pivotal role leaders play in cultivating, nurturing, and evolving organizational cultures.

Southwest Airlines, under the leadership of Herb Kelleher, provides an inspiring example of how a leader can influence organizational culture. While other airlines were laying off employees during difficult times, Kelleher made the bold decision to avoid layoffs in 2000 by encouraging employees to be a part of the solution and help save money. In 2012, Southwest Airlines once again asked its employees to help it stay competitive by finding ways to save $5 a day, repeating an initiative used by then-Chief Executive Officer Herb Kelleher in 2000, when the airline's fuel costs rose 63 percent. Employees responded to their leader's call and his plan worked. No one was laid off. [7] This commitment to employees and the organization's culture of love led to remarkable financial turnaround and long-term profitability. The ticker symbol for Southwest airlines, LUV says it all.

Chick-fil-A is renowned for its culture of exceptional customer service, genuine hospitality, and strong values epitomized by the words "My pleasure." For organizations like Chick-fil-A, many people, especially their employees, wholeheartedly connect with their values. **When an organization's values align with someone's personal values, a powerful bond is formed**. This commitment to values was evident from the early days when the founder, Truett Cathy, made a bold decision for one of the first Chick-fil-A restaurants to be located within a mall. Despite the prevailing notion that opening on Sundays was crucial for profits, Cathy prioritized taking care of his employees and staying true to his values. His decision to close on Sundays, despite potential profit losses, exemplifies the importance of aligning culture with core values. Those who share the same values will respect such decisions manifested by customer loyalty. This core value is deeply ingrained in Chick-fil-A's culture, which is truly remarkable. Prior to my military retirement, several officers from the Air War College visited the Chick-Fil-A headquarters in Atlanta, GA to discuss culture with one of their senior executives, Mark Miller, author of the new book, *Culture Rules*. Our visit was inspiring. They do not hide behind their culture; it is on full display. Chick-fil-A remains unapologetically true to who they are. One striking symbol of their commitment to servant leadership is the bronze statue of Jesus washing a disciple's feet. This statue encapsulates their unwavering dedication to serving others and exemplifies their core values ("We're here to serve"). Chick-fil-A's commitment to servant leadership and community involvement has earned them a devoted following and sustained success. Not everyone will agree with or support Chick-fil-A's beliefs. People have the freedom to voice their differing beliefs and opinions by working or eating elsewhere; however, it is undeniable that Chick-fil-A has cultivated an extraordinary culture rooted in their values and a genuine commitment to servant leadership. To this day, the long hiring process for operations managers culminates with a signing ceremony in Truett Cathy's old office symbolizing how the strong values of Truett Cathy remain the core values for the company he created.

Decoding Culture

There are two noteworthy books that provide valuable insights on culture. One of them, *Organizational Culture and Leadership*, written by Dr. Edgar Schein, is highly regarded in academic settings as research that captures the essence of organizational culture. According to Schein, culture is composed of patterns of shared basic assumptions that are deeply ingrained, often unconsciously. These assumptions shape our identity and define how we operate. [8] Another remarkable book is Simon Sinek's *Leaders Eat Last*, which further emphasizes the essence of culture, deriving the title of his book from his observations of Marine Corps culture in action. Sinek emphasizes that culture is manifested in the way things truly get done. [9] Have you ever experienced joining a new organization, eagerly familiarizing yourself with the policies and guidelines, only to discover on your first day that reality operates differently? It is a common occurrence, especially in military culture where policies may take a backseat to actual practice. This intriguing observation sheds light on culture's essence and how it drives organizations. When assessing the strength of a culture, particularly as a newcomer, observe how decisions are made and where people find safety. If conformity to rules and regulations takes precedence, it may indicate a culture focused on doing things "by the book," which runs counter to an organization that values innovation and "outside the box" thinking. How many times have you encountered automated workers asserting, "I'm sorry, I can't assist you" or "the computer won't let me…"? Personally, it frustrates me to no end when confronted with such situations. I would rather engage with a human being who possesses the flexibility to help beyond the confines of rigid protocols.

  Strong cultures, on the other hand, derive strength from relationships. They prioritize people and extend themselves to provide support and assistance. Relationships matter. For example, the phrases most heard at Publix and Chick Fil-A are

"How may I help you," and "My pleasure." In a strong culture, individuals willingly admit their knowledge gaps and seek guidance from their peers. They foster a mentorship-oriented climate. Does your organization lean more towards being rules-based or relationships-based?

22. Describe your organizational culture.

_____
_____
_____
_____
_____
_____
_____
_____
_____
_____
_____
_____
_____
_____
_____
_____
_____
_____

When Cultures Collide

When clashes between cultures occur, the consequences can be severe. This notion was brought to my attention during a recent conversation with my wife concerning the fate of Gimbal's jellybeans. To my dismay, she informed me that the company had been acquired, resulting in a gradual erosion of the quality once embodied by the Gimbal's brand. The organizational culture which made Gimbal's had been supplanted by the new company's culture which fundamentally changed the original product. My wife, sadly, no longer purchases Gimbal's jellybeans. This situation resonated with me on a personal level as I reflected upon the experiences of my own brothers, who have witnessed the detrimental effects of talent being stifled within organizations following an acquisition. It serves as a stark reminder of the potential ramifications when distinct cultures collide resulting in a new culture.

This raises an intriguing question: Have you witnessed the collision of two organizations with fundamentally different cultures attempting to work together?

23. Describe a time you observed a collision of cultures.

Such occurrences are not uncommon and often present significant challenges. A notable book on leadership by General Mattis, the former Secretary of Defense, provides valuable insights into this topic. In *Call Sign CHAOS, Learning to Lead*, Mattis candidly recounts his struggle to define policy and develop strategies aligned with both military and National Security objectives. The Air War College teaches senior military officers and national security officials the importance of understanding the desired end state outlined by the national command authorities (the President and Secretary of Defense). However, throughout his extensive career spanning three decades and multiple administrations, General Mattis seldom encountered a clear overall vision from these top-level decision-makers. This absence necessitated the creation of strategic plans in a void, resulting in collisions when attempting to align disparate perspectives and interests. [10]

Navigating such collisions requires effective communication, dialogue, and discourse to arrive at optimal solutions. This process can be arduous, as different stakeholders possess distinct perspectives, values, and priorities. Complicating matters further, military strategists are inclined to present limited options, often favoring a single preferred course of action, which may not align with the broader spectrum of decision-making requirements for multiple options. It is essential to recognize the need for patience and an openness to find common ground. Despite the challenges, constructive discourse fosters the emergence of viable solutions, steering organizations toward successful outcomes. Any variance in interpretation can give rise to friction or the development of microcultures. While it may be challenging to reconcile this divergence, it is crucial to respect and value differing perspectives. In so doing, we cultivate a dynamic culture that accommodates a range of perspectives while upholding our shared values.

Collisions between organizational cultures demand careful navigation and a commitment to effective communication. The consequences of cultural clashes can be far-reaching, impacting the essence of a brand or stifling the talent within an organization. However, leaders can mitigate the challenges that arise when cultures collide by fostering an open dialogue, patience, and a willingness to find consensus. Embracing diversity of thought and encouraging individuals to find alignment with shared values strengthens the fabric of our organizational cultures and propels us toward collective success.

Artifacts, Beliefs, and Assumptions

Dr. Edgar Schein provides valuable insights into understanding and defining culture. According to his extensive research, culture can be examined through three distinct layers: artifacts, beliefs, and assumptions. **Artifacts** represent the visible aspects of culture that lie above the waterline, such as the way we dress, symbols, or tangible items like company uniforms. These artifacts are observable manifestations of culture.

Moving below the waterline, we encounter the underlying elements that truly shape a culture. **Norms and values** form the core of an organization's culture. Although intangible, they are powerful forces that guide behavior, inform decision-making, and reflect what an organization believes in. These norms and values are often explicitly articulated, such as in the form of a creed or set of shared principles or beliefs that define the organization's identity. Deeper still are the **underlying assumptions** that form the bedrock of a culture. These assumptions are deeply ingrained and may not be explicitly stated or easily described. They are fundamental beliefs and paradigms that influence how the team functions and behaves. These underlying assumptions govern the way things are done within the organization, shaping its distinctive character. [11]

Dr. Schein's comprehensive framework provides a holistic understanding of culture, encompassing both the visible artifacts and the invisible, yet powerful, dimensions of beliefs and assumptions. By examining these layers, leaders can gain profound insights into their organization's culture, enabling them to align values, drive behavior, and shape the desired organizational identity. It is through a comprehensive examination of these elements that leaders can effectively cultivate and nurture a thriving organizational culture.

Organizational Climate

Organizational climate, often referred to as command climate in military terminology, plays a crucial role in shaping the values, priorities, and expectations within an organization. It is akin to the atmosphere that permeates the organization, giving insights into what the organization values and what it does not. Allow me to illustrate this concept through a personal experience during one of my command assignments.

Upon assuming my role as commanding officer, I decided to maintain the current "battle rhythm" which included weekly staff meetings every Tuesday at 9am. Being someone who values punctuality and understands the importance of respecting everyone else's time, I arrived at the meeting room five minutes early. To my surprise, people were still trickling in 15 minutes after the scheduled start time. Feeling the need to address this issue, I gathered everyone's attention by closing the door and expressing my displeasure. I later learned that the previous commander was habitually 15 minutes late to his own staff meeting, thus bad habits of tardiness became the norm for everyone. In other words, a climate of poor punctuality had become the norm.

Culture

During that pivotal moment, I emphasized the significance of punctuality, acknowledging the value of my time as well as that of each individual present. I made it clear that punctuality would be expected henceforth. From that point forward, arriving five minutes early became the expectation, and no one was late again. It was essential for me to establish a new norm, as the previous commander had allowed tardiness to persist without consequences.

While some may argue that such a change could have been allowed to be slowly corrected over many meetings, the urgency of the situation demanded immediate action to reinforce the desired command climate. My role as the leader meant it was my responsibility to transform the climate by instilling punctuality as a core organizational value which happened instantly.

This example highlights the malleability of organizational climate and how leaders can swiftly impact and redefine it. Changing the climate does not require drastic measures. Effective communication, coupled with setting clear expectations and standards, can significantly influence the desired organizational climate.

By addressing issues that hinder productivity or compromise values, leaders can mold a climate that aligns with the organization's vision and fosters a positive and effective work environment.

This anecdote underscores the importance of recognizing and intentionally shaping the organizational climate, as it directly influences employee behavior, morale, and overall performance. Leaders have the power to reshape the climate, even in the face of well-established norms. By aligning the climate with the organization's values and goals, leaders can create an environment conducive to success, where punctuality and other desired behaviors are not only encouraged but embodied by all employees as an organizational norm.

Cultural Communications

Effective communication within organizations is a multifaceted process that encompasses various elements, including the use of metaphors and specialized language. Military jargon often takes on a unique form of communication, characterized by acronyms and internal references unknown to those not in uniform. For instance, calling someone a "shipmate" can carry different meanings depending on the context and tone. It can be a term of camaraderie or, conversely, an expression of disapproval. Similarly, lighthearted slogans like "Go Army, Beat Navy" exemplify the playful rivalry between different branches of the armed forces. Anyone who knows me understands how I love to belt out "YUT" for no reason other than to express my motivation for whatever the task in front of us may be. This is a phrase from the Marine Corps which loosely translates into "Yelling Useless Things," but for me, it is all about offering a motivational greeting or to inspire. Jargon even exists among other Universities. I suspect many of you have witnessed someone belt out "War Eagle" to a stranger simply because they were wearing the iconic AU or Auburn on their hat or shirt. Each of those greetings typically results in a conversation about our beloved alma mater.

24. Does your organization communicate in any unique ways?

Metaphors and specialized language serve as powerful tools for expressing shared experiences and reinforcing the sense of community within an organization. They create a common language that facilitates communication among members who understand the underlying meanings and cultural references. These linguistic devices not only convey information but also emotions, values, and identity.

Organizations should be mindful that effective communication goes beyond the use of metaphors and specialized language. It involves employing clear and concise language, active listening, and adapting communication styles to suit different audiences and contexts. Open and transparent communication channels should be established to foster an environment where ideas can be freely shared, concerns can be addressed, and feedback can be given constructively.

Organizations should also embrace diverse communication mediums, such as face-to-face interactions, written communication, and digital platforms, to cater to different communication preferences to enhance understanding. This is especially true in organizations where multiple generations work together to achieve the same organizational goals. Regular and structured communication, including team meetings, newsletters, and progress reports, can ensure that relevant information is disseminated efficiently and consistently. By embracing diverse communication methods and fostering open channels for dialogue, organizations can cultivate an environment where effective communication thrives, enabling collaboration, understanding, and success.

Notes:

1. Peter Drucker. Culture eats strategy is attributed to comments made by Peter Drucker in 2006.
2. Publix overview and culture. https://corporate.publix.com/about-publix.
3. Wal-Mart purpose. https://corporate.walmart.com/purpose.
4. Mike Jernigan. *Auburn Man, The Life and Times of George Petrie*. The Donnell Group. Montgomery, AL. 2007.
5. Ibid.
6. Jim Collins. *Good to Great*. Why Some Companies Make the Leap and Others Don't. Harper Business. New York, New York. 2001.
7. SFGate. "Southwest Airlines Asks its Employees for Ideas." https://www.sfgate.com/business/article/southwest-asks-its-employees-for-ideas-3805398.php
8. Edgar Schein. *Organizational Culture and Leadership*. Jossey-Bass. San Francisco, CA. 2010.
9. Simon Sinek. Leaders Eat Last. Portfolio Publishers. New York, New York. 2014.
10. Jim Mattis. *Call Sign Chaos: Learning to Lead*. Random House. Manhattan, New York. 2019.
11. Edgar Schein. *Organizational Culture and Leadership*. Jossey-Bass. San Francisco, CA. 2010.

Marine Corps Culture

Chapter Ten

Marine Corps Culture

Marine Corps culture is a tapestry woven with rich traditions and deeply ingrained values. In this chapter, we will explore the essence of Marine Corps culture, specifically, the artifacts, core values, and hidden assumptions which collectively make the Marine Corps one of the most respected and feared fighting organizations in the world. From ribbons and haircuts to acts of selflessness and heroism, the Marine Corps culture embodies a unique mindset that drives its members to excel. By examining the defining elements of this remarkable culture, we can glean valuable insights and lessons for leadership in any organization. Specifically, Dr. Schein's theory on culture allows us to analyze and better understand the Marine Corps.

For example, several artifacts are present in my last official Marine Corps photograph. Those **artifacts** are my ribbons, haircut, rank insignia, form-fitting uniform, American and Marine Corps flags, and even my smile. These are all artifacts. You see them. They mean something. Each artifact tells a story, representing achievements, experiences, even personality. From the vibrant ribbons denoting meritorious service to the insignia of rank proudly displayed, these artifacts hold deep meaning for Marines. Notably, the regulation haircut serves as a visual identifier, symbolizing discipline, and adherence to standards. Even after retirement, the impact of these artifacts lingers since they were ingrained in the very fabric of my personal identity. Eighteen months into military retirement, my wife takes pleasure in me not having to maintain a Marine Corps regulation haircut, although I still prefer my old hair style.

Marine Corps Culture

At the heart of Marine Corps culture lie three core **values**: honor, courage, and commitment. These values form the bedrock of every Marine's character, shaping their actions and decisions. Violating any of these values is inconceivable, leading to the swift end of one's military service. Such deeply held beliefs inspire a warrior ethos that drives Marines to embrace uncertainty, confront adversity, and commit to excellence and innovation.

Beneath the surface of Marine Corps culture lies a set of **hidden assumptions** that govern how things are done. A poignant example of this is the practice of "leaders eat last." Though never explicitly stated in policy or formal training, this unspoken principle exemplifies servant leadership. Marine leaders prioritize the needs of their subordinates, ensuring their well-being before their own. This selfless mentality reinforces the bond of trust and fosters a culture of care and support.

I will always remember my initial experience in a deployed exercise, where all the officers gathered in a tent for our staff meeting prior to dinner. As the meeting ended, the anticipation of my next meal grew as did a long line of Marines eagerly waiting outside. When the chow line finally opened, I stood up, ready to satisfy my hunger; however, a Captain promptly grabbed my arm and sternly told me, **"Lieutenant, leaders eat last. Take a seat."** It was an unwritten rule, not explicitly outlined in any policy or taught during officer training at the basic school. Reluctantly, I sat there, watching each Marine pass through the line. Eventually, the officers rose and made their way to the end of the line with me following. By the time I reached the food, it had turned cold, but I was grateful to finally eat. Then, I realized why leaders eat last. Our responsibility is to those Marines entrusted to our care. As such, we should ensure they are properly fed with a warm meal even if that means we forego such comforts. That is our job as Marine Corps leaders. **This was my first lesson in servant leadership, prioritizing the well-being of those under our care.** Even now, as a retired Marine, you will likely find me at the end of the chow line. Old habits die hard; however, this mindset reflects the importance of ensuring the welfare of others, and I happily accept it.

Several years later during a deployment to the Middel East, I—along with the other five officers—was offered an air-conditioned room on a base in the middle of nowhere. We politely turned down the generous offer, instead choosing to remain with the other 130 Marines under our care, even though that meant living in open concrete squad bays with no air conditioning. We never thought twice about our decision; that is simply who we are. **Leaders eat last.**

A defining aspect (**assumption**) of Marine Corps culture is the unwavering commitment to leave no one behind. This principle applies not only on the battlefield but permeates all levels of the organization. The story of Dakota Meyer, a Congressional Medal of Honor recipient, vividly illustrates this commitment. His Medal of Honor citation is awe inspiring.

Corporal Meyer maintained security at a patrol rally point while other members of his team moved on foot with two platoons of Afghan National Army and Border Police into the village of Ganjgal for a pre-dawn meeting with village elders. Moving into the village, the patrol was ambushed by more than 50 enemy fighters firing rocket propelled grenades, mortars, and machine guns from houses and fortified positions on the slopes above. Hearing over the radio that four U.S. team members were cut off, Corporal Meyer seized the initiative. With a fellow Marine driving, Corporal Meyer took the exposed gunner's position in a gun-truck as they drove down the steeply terraced terrain in a daring attempt to disrupt the enemy attack and locate the trapped U.S. team. Disregarding intense enemy fire now concentrated on their lone vehicle, Corporal Meyer killed a number of enemy fighters with the mounted machine guns and his rifle, some at near point-blank range, as he and his driver made three solo trips into the ambush area. During the first two trips, he and his driver evacuated two dozen Afghan soldiers, many of whom were wounded. When one machine gun became inoperable, he directed a return to the rally point to switch to another gun-truck for a third trip into the ambush area where his accurate fire directly supported the remaining U.S. personnel and Afghan soldiers fighting their way out of the ambush. Despite a shrapnel wound to his arm, Corporal Meyer made two more trips into the ambush area in a third gun-truck accompanied by four other Afghan vehicles to recover more wounded Afghan soldiers and search for the missing U.S. team members. Still under heavy enemy fire, he dismounted the vehicle on the fifth trip and moved on foot to locate and recover the bodies of his team members. Corporal Meyer's daring initiative and bold fighting spirit throughout the 6-hour battle significantly disrupted the enemy's attack and inspired the members of the combined force to fight on. His unwavering courage and steadfast devotion to his U.S. and Afghan comrades in the face of almost certain death reflected great credit upon himself and upheld the highest traditions of the Marine Corps and the United States Naval Service. [1]

Despite overwhelming odds, then-Corporal Meyer repeatedly risked his life to rescue fallen comrades. His words to CBS News Correspondent David Martin in a "60 Minutes" interview when asked if he was concerned about being killed were simply, "I didn't think I was going to die, I knew it...There was U.S. troops getting shot at and those are your brothers." For Meyer, the mission was clear. "You either get them out alive or you die trying. If you don't die trying, you didn't try hard enough." [2] His actions epitomize the selflessness and dedication that define the underlying assumption to leave no one behind that defines Marine Corps culture. No one ordered him to rush into the kill zone to get to his brothers-in-arms, he just did so, without much thought. In fact, he did so after several requests for fire support went unanswered. That is the remarkable power culture can have on an individual.

Dining Out

In a captivating display of tradition and camaraderie, I had the privilege to serve as the guest speaker during a unit "Dining Out" event with 3rd Low Altitude Air Defense (LAAD) Battalion in San Diego, CA—captured in the photograph on the following page. The allure of a Dining Out lies in the adherence to a set of time-honored rules, failure to comply resulting in drinking from the infamous "grog," a concoction most would rather avoid due to its unpleasant taste. Nonetheless, it is an integral part of the experience, one that epitomizes a sense of shared commitment and camaraderie.

During this event, I shared a poignant speech that conjured images of the legendary Battle of Belleau Wood and the indomitable spirit of Marine Corps hero Gunnery Sergeant Dan Daly. To accentuate the gravity of the moment, I unveiled bottles of water procured from the revered fountain at Belleau Wood, imbued with the myth that drinking from it bestows immortality in combat. With a bit of drama befitting the moment, I poured every drop of this sacred water into the grog, declaring, "May you never die in combat." The room erupted with a collective gasp, punctuating the profound significance of the gesture.

The culmination of my speech sparked a spirited rush among the 350 Marines present, eager to consume the grog as swiftly as possible. Even my wife was happy to join in the endeavor and embrace the spirit of unity. **This shared experience served as a testament to the power of culture and tradition, where myths and stories intertwine to reinforce our collective identity.** This memorable Dining Out was a toast to our vibrant culture, a poignant reminder that our shared narratives and rituals forge unbreakable bonds that strengthen our warrior ethos.

The Unbreakable Jack Lucas

Allow me to introduce you to Jack Lucas, an extraordinary American hero whose story embodies the spirit of courage, selflessness, and sacrifice. In 1942, at the young age of 14, Jack displayed an unwavering devotion to his country by forging his mother's signature so he could enlist in the Marine Corps (parents' consent was required for those under 18). Driven by a profound love for our country, he yearned to fight for what he believed in.

Three years later, Jack found himself on the treacherous battlefield of Iwo Jima, amidst the horrors of war. In a small bunker with three other Marines, two enemy grenades abruptly descended upon them. Without a moment's hesitation, Jack selflessly threw himself on both grenades. He swiftly pushed one grenade into the sand with the buttstock of his weapon while pulling the second grenade under his chest thereby, shielding his comrades from harm. Though the explosion sent him flying several feet, Jack's bravery saved the lives of those alongside him. [3] Initially presumed dead, his resilient spirit prevailed, and he defied the odds by surviving the battle where "Uncommon valor was common virtue." [4]

At the astonishing age of 17, Jacklyn "Jack" Lucas became the third youngest recipient of the Medal of Honor in our nation's history, forever etching his name into the fabric of our great nation. Of note, the two youngest were awarded the Medal of Honor during the Civil War.

For conspicuous gallantry and intrepidity at the risk of his life above and beyond the call of duty while serving with the 1st Battalion, 26th Marines, 5th Marine Division, during action against enemy Japanese forces on Iwo Jima, Volcano Islands, 20 February 1945. While creeping through a treacherous, twisting ravine which ran in close proximity to a fluid and uncertain front line on D-day plus one, Pfc. Lucas and three other men were suddenly ambushed by a hostile patrol which savagely attacked with rifle fire and grenades. Quick to act when the lives of the small group were endangered by two grenades which landed directly in front of them, Pfc. Lucas unhesitatingly hurled himself over his comrades upon one grenade and pulled the other under him, absorbing the whole blasting forces of the explosions in his own body in order to shield his companions from the concussion and murderous flying fragments. By his inspiring action and valiant spirit of self-sacrifice, he not only protected his comrades from certain injury or possible death but also enabled them to rout the

Japanese patrol and continue the advance. His exceptionally courageous initiative and loyalty reflect the highest credit upon Pfc. Lucas and the U.S. Naval Service. [5]

His story embodies the essence of Marine Corps culture as one that reveres valor, selflessness, and the unwavering determination to protect others. In 2010, I found myself aboard the USS *Iwo Jima*, named after the iconic battle, that forever linked Jack Lucas to Marine Corps legacy. Near the end of our deployment, we had a final planned port-call in Cuba. The day prior would find us just off the coast, a beautiful scene for our planned commemoration of the Marine Corps' birthday. I had planned a stirring speech centered on our successful actions throughout our deployment when I was stopped by a Navy Chief Warrant Officer who was eager to show me a challenge coin. He asked if I knew the name engraved on the coin to which I said, "Of course, Jack Lucas is a hero. Our flight deck above is even named after him." His response was, "Jack Lucas was my grandfather-in-law." I listened intently as the officer told me how Jack Lucas was allowed to visit the USS Iwo Jima multiple times during construction and on his final visit, just before the ship's hull was sealed, Jack Lucas entered the belly of the ship and placed his Medal of Honor on the hull, thereby making it a permanent fixture within the mighty

Amphibious ship. Upon inquiry, I learned that no one on board knew this incredible story or that a family member connected to our legacy was assigned to the ship.

I implored the officer to allow me to share this remarkable connection. He initially hesitated, humbly reluctant to bring attention to his family's connection; however, understanding the magnitude of this untold story, he agreed to be recognized for his lineage to a genuine hero. The following day, with the ship's Commander unaware of the tale that would soon unfold, the Navy Chief Warrant Officer was seated in the front row, replacing the customary position reserved for the commanding officer. As I commenced my speech, I disregarded my original prepared remarks, choosing instead to recount the remarkable legacy of Jack Lucas, the Medal of Honor permanently sealed inside our ship, and the family connection for one of the ship's permanently assigned officers. Emotions ran high, and not a dry eye could be found among those in the front row, captivated by the power of our shared narrative.

This poignant event left an indelible mark. While some may have been initially puzzled by the Navy officer's prominent seat, they soon understood the profound significance behind it. Our story, our culture, is defined by such extraordinary individuals and their selfless acts of heroism and the Chief Warrant Officer was the living manifestation of our legacy.

Myths, Legends, and Legacy

Marine Corps culture thrives on its myths, legends, and heritage. These stories, passed down through generations, forge a shared identity and foster a sense of pride. The enduring legacy of heroes like Dakota Meyer, Dan Daly, and Jack Lucas embody the Marine Corps spirit. They instill a sense of purpose and remind Marines of the extraordinary feats achieved by those who have gone before us in service to our country.

Understanding Marine Corps culture offers valuable insights for leaders in any organization. The artifacts, values, hidden assumptions, and narratives that comprise this unique culture demonstrate the power of shared identity and unwavering commitment to a set of values and beliefs. By embracing the principles of honor, courage, commitment, and by fostering a servant leadership mentality, Marine Corps leaders cultivate a culture of excellence, resilience, and selflessness. Marine Corps culture serves as a testament to the transformative potential strong values, legacy, and selfless service can have on organizations.

Now, as we approach the culmination of our journey together, I invite you to reflect on your own culture. Take a moment to define the essence of your organizational identity. Consider the artifacts, values, and assumptions that shape who you are as a team.

25. What Artifacts does your organization have?

_____
_____
_____
_____
_____
_____
_____
_____
_____

26. What are your organization's values, beliefs, and norms?

_____
_____
_____
_____
_____
_____
_____
_____
_____
_____
_____

27. What are your organization's underlying assumptions?

_____
_____
_____
_____
_____
_____
_____
_____
_____
_____
_____
_____

Finding Your Personal Culture

We think of culture in terms of organizations, yet have you ever paused to consider the concept of personal culture or how culture can apply to individuals? Contemplating this notion can lead to profound self-reflection, unlocking valuable insights to who we truly are. **All 30 of your entries in this book will help you discover your values, ethics, character, and leadership philosophy. Combined, these aspects make up your personal culture.** This introspective journey not only helps us truly know who we are, but also helps us cultivate our own culture so we can lead and inspire with authenticity.

Several years ago, while teaching culture at the Air War College, I thought it would be an interesting project to craft my own culture. The results were quite helpful in articulating to others who I truly am. For example, **my artifacts** include a cross, the Marine Corps logo, the Auburn University logo, pictures of an author, an instructor, a husband and a father, a reader, and a traveler. **My beliefs** include my personal values of integrity, faith, family, teamwork, communication, commitment, loyalty, humility, relationships. Finally, **my basic underlying assumption** is an unyielding foundation—**character**. Derived from the Greek word "char," meaning to engrave, character forms an indelible imprint on our being. Just as a stone bears the mark of its engraver, our character shapes the essence of who we are—a steadfast presence that remains resolute and unchanging. **This profound realization serves as my hidden assumption, a guiding force that breathes life into my values and beliefs.**

Following my freshman year at Auburn, I closed out my checking account before catching a bus from Auburn, Alabama to Dallas, Texas (to live with my uncle who had set up a summer job for me). I'll never forget the bank teller who laughed when I asked to close my account. I asked, what is so funny? She said, "you only have .97 cents." I suppose a deep-seated

Personal Culture

assumption I have based on that experience is hard work and wise investments. I promised myself that I would never be that broke again. That small nest egg has grown but only through strong commitment to my values, beliefs, and underlying assumption of character and hard work.

Reflecting on this exploration, we are reminded of the power of authenticity. Authenticity allows us to challenge conventions, to embrace our true selves, and to celebrate the unique aspects that make us who we are. In a world where conformity often prevails, let us find the courage to smile, to respect others, build bridges and meaningful relationships, to be unapologetically ourselves, and to chart our own paths, adhering to our unique leadership philosophy derived through crucibles that taught us our values, virtue, ethics, and character. Now, it is your turn to embark on this voyage of self-discovery. Take a moment to reflect, to select the artifacts that define your identity, beliefs, and values. As you do so, seek to unveil the underlying foundational assumption that propels you. Using Dr. Schein's analysis of culture, craft your own personal culture.

28. What are your personal Artifacts?

_____
_____
_____
_____

29. What are your personal Beliefs/Values?

30. What is your underlying assumption?

In Closing

I sincerely hope you have been encouraged by taking this leadership journey with me and that you have not only been inspired to lead with a higher purpose, but also inspired to earn invisible medals. **Invisible medals** will be earned if we focus on people and relationships, view life as a stewardship, and recognize that everyone has potential. Remember that giving invisible medals is equally important as earning them.

Everyone has a purpose. Finding one's **purpose** and **story** comes from life's lessons, **crucibles** (challenges), and deep self-**reflection**.

Everyone can be a leader, but leading with a higher purpose requires us to embody our **values**, make sound ethical decisions, and display consistent **character**. These qualities help us overcome the **crucibles** (challenges) we face in life, enabling us to serve and inspire others to lead…to earn invisible medals.

The takeaway from this journey has been self-discovery and understanding how your personal values form your core **leadership philosophy** upon which all aspects of your leadership potential can be unleashed. We defined powerful values essential to becoming an extraordinary leader, uplifting others, and being a leader worthy of invisible medals. We explored virtues and Dr. Kem's ethical triangle (principle, consequence, and virtue). This framework helps us make decisions even when faced with unfavorable options. Remember, character is developed through our everyday actions (President Reagan's quote). Our actions either strengthen or damage our character, so it is crucial to be mindful of our actions, recognizing that we are always on full display.

Organizational **culture** runs deep, driven by intangible attributes. The same applies to individuals. That is why I encouraged you to reflect on your **personal culture**. Sometimes we do not even realize why we think the way we do until we take a deep dive and uncover our true selves.

Leading with a higher purpose and a desire to earn invisible medals requires us to live with intentional awareness of our personal values and a commitment to a moral and ethical code of conduct. By living intentionally, we develop habits that reflect our character. Leaders with character earn the respect of their teams and can cultivate a strong organizational culture based on trust and meaningful relationships. Once you know yourself in this way, you have reached the highest level of development—self-actualization—enabling you to create your own leadership philosophy and set out to positively impact other people by helping them also achieve self-actualization.

Lastly, I want to share a thought-provoking quote from Peter Drucker on destiny. [6]

Watch your thoughts, for they become your words. Choose your words, for they become your actions. Understand your actions, for they become habits. Study your habits, for they will become your character. Develop your character, for it will become your destiny.

Best of luck on your continued leadership journey!

I hope you earn countless invisible medals along the way…

C. S. Richie
Colonel, USMC (Retired)
Humble servant

Notes:

1. Sergeant Dakota Myer Medal of Honor citation.
https://www.cmohs.org/recipients/dakota-l-meyer
2. CBS News. https://www.cbsnews.com/news/medal-of-honor-recipient-dakota-meyer-on-60-minutes/
3. Jack Lucas. Indestructible: The Unforgettable Memoir of a Marine Hero at the Battle of Iwo Jima. Da Capo Press. Lebanon, Indiana. 2006.
4. Admiral Chester Nimitz famous quote referring to the men who fought on Iwo Jima.
5. Jack Lucas Medal of Honor citation.
https://www.cmohs.org/recipients/jacklyn-h-lucas
6. Peter Drucker has often been attributed as the author who first spoke this quote on character.

Appendix 1: Questions for Reflection

1. What would you like people to say about you as their leader?

2. Have you earned any Invisible Medals by positively influencing another human being? If so, who was it and what did you do for them?

3. Has anyone done something for you that positively impacted your life?

4. Have you ever helped someone overcome a hardship or achieve a goal? How did it make you feel?

5. Who has influenced your life or helped you discover your purpose?

6. What events or people inspired you to become the person you are or hope to be?

7. Have you discovered your purpose? If so, what is it?

8. Tell me about yourself (i.e. your elevator speech)?

9. Have you experienced any life crucibles? What were they and what did you learn about yourself?

10. What is your leadership philosophy?

11. What is your definition of leadership?

12. Who comes to mind when you think of a good leader you Have known? What leadership traits did they embody?

13. What type of leader are you?

14. Why is murder universally regarded as wrong?

15. What are your personal values?

16. What are your team's values?

17. Identify times when you failed. What did you learn about yourself?

18. Have you ever experienced an ethical dilemma? What did you learn about yourself (your values, virtue, ethics)?

19. If you were a member of the advisory group, what would you have recommended and why? If you were President Truman, would you have made the same decision?

20. Think of a time when you were a member of a high-performing team. What were the characteristics of that of the leader?

21. Identify the Differences between Wal-Mart and Publix

22. Describe your organizational culture.

23. Describe a time you observed a collision of cultures.

24. Does your organization communicate in any unique ways?

25. What Artifacts does your organization have?

26. What are your organization's values, beliefs, and norms?

27. What are your organization's underlying assumptions?

28. What are your personal Artifacts?

29. What are your personal Beliefs/Values?

30. What is your underlying assumption?

Appendix 2: Additional Notes and Reflection

About the Author

Colonel Chris Richie, Marine Corps (Retired), is the Director, Auburn University Human Resource Development, and a leadership instructor for the Harbert College of Business.

From 2018-2022, he was on faculty at the Air War College as the Marine Corps Advisor, an instructor in the Department of Leadership, and a board member for the Alabama Military Hall of Honor.

During a military career spanning three decades, Chris led teams and organizations ranging in size from 35 to 2,500 people. He commanded the largest Aviation Command and Control (AC2) organization in the Marine Corps and holds the distinction as the only AC2 officer to command a Special Purpose Marine Air Ground Task Force. He served in 20 countries, leading thousands of people around the globe in times of peace and war. The Executive Steering Committee Chairman for the Marine Corps AC2 community (a worldwide organization exceeding 10,000 people), Chris also served as a diplomat in the United Arab Emirates as military liaison to the U.S. Ambassador and Emirati Armed Forces.

Chris is a 3-time award-winning leadership author, an Amazon best seller/#1 new release, and essay winner for the inaugural Colin Powell Joint Warfighting essay contest. The 2003 AC2 Marine Corps Officer of the Year and commander of the 2010 AC2 Marine Corps Unit of the year, he has taught leadership at the University level since 2018, was recognized as a 2021 Air War College Instructor of the year and the 2022 Director's award recipient for outstanding Servant Leadership. Chris earned the Defense Superior Service Medal, Legion of Merit, ten meritorious service and achievement medals, and multiple service awards while supporting several humanitarian and combat operations around the globe. His most valued medal is the Invisible Medal, earned when you positively impact another person's life.

Chris is a member of the Auburn NROTC Alumni Board of Directors, Vice President for the East Alabama chapter of the Military Officer's Association of America, member of the AU Credit Union supervisory committee, and a regular keynote speaker.

www.theinvisiblemedal.com

www.linkedin.com/in/chris-richie-usmc